The Bronze Bow

A guide to Elizabeth George Speare's novel
by
Shan Gillard

ISBN: 1477656618
ISBN-13: 978-1477656617

DEDICATION

For all those parents and teachers who desire to teach the truth of salvation to their children.

TABLE OF CONTENTS

AUTHOR BIOGRAPHY

Born in Melrose, Massachusetts on November 21, 1908 to Harry Allan and Demetria George, Elizabeth George Speare spent a happy childhood in New England with her parents and younger brother. Her summers, spent at the beach with her family in an area where there were no other young people, gave her the opportunity to develop a lifelong love of reading, and helped to shape the imagination that would later serve to create the award winning children's stories she would write. Although she began writing at the age of eight, and wrote stories all through high school, she did not pursue writing as a career until much later in her life. Speare received her Bachelor of Arts degree from Smith College in 1930, then went on to earn a master's degree in English from Boston University. From 1932 to 1936 she taught high school English in several private high schools in Massachusetts. She particularly enjoyed this, stating, "it was always a thrill to watch some girl or boy discover for the first time te enchantment of reading and writing." She spent her vacations as a camp counselor, and one summer traveling in Europe.

In 1936 she married Alden Speare, and they settled in Connecticut, where their two children were born. For the next several years Speare was absorbed in the activities of her children, delighting herself in her role of mother. When both of her children entered junior high, she began to once again take up the activity of writing. She began with publishing articles in women's magazines. While researching the history of New England, Speare came upon the story of a young girl who was captured by Indians during the French and Indian War. From this, she developed her first novel, *Calico Captive*, which was published in 1957. Her second book, *The Witch of Blackbird Pond*, was published in 1958 and won the Newbery Medal in 1959. *The Bronze Bow*, the only book which she set outside of New England, was published in 1961, and also earned a Newbery Medal. *The Sign of the Beaver* was published in 1984, and won a Newbery Honor Citation, the Scott O'Dell Award for Historical Fiction, and the Christopher award. Speare received the Laura Ingalls Wilder Award for her distinguished and enduring contribution to children's literature in 1989.

Elizabeth George Speare died of an aortic aneurysm on November 15, 1994, at the age of 86. Because of her contribution to children's literature, she was also named to the Educational Paperback Association's list of the 100 Best Selling Children's Authors of all time.

BACKGROUND INFORMATION

Intertestament Period:

In order to fully understand the depth of Daniel's emotion in the story, it is necessary to have at least a surface understanding of the history of the people of Israel, and particularly those living in Galilee during the time leading up to the life of Christ. After the Jews returned from Babylonian exile, they rebuilt the Temple in Jerusalem in 515 BC, and were allowed religious and political autonomy until the rise of the Greek empire in the fourth century BC. When Alexander the Great conquered the known world, the spread of the Greek language and the Greek culture affected the Israelites just as it did every other nation in existence at that period of time. The Hasidim or "Pious Ones" developed as a reaction against the Hellenization of Jewish culture. They refused to have anything to do with that which was not clean under the Jewish law. There were divisions among the Hasidim that led to the development of the Pharisees, the Sadducees, the Essenes and the Zealots.

After Alexander's death, his empire was divided into four parts. Syria and Egypt were constantly fighting over Palestine, causing the area to remain in turmoil. In the second century BC, the Syrian Seleucids gained power, and Antiochus III defeated the Ptolemies of Egypt, driving them out of Palestine and taking control of the area. His son, Antiochus IV Epiphanes desecrated the Temple and effectively forced paganism on the Jews. Twice he plundered the Temple.

Although many of the Jews went along with the liberal, worldly beliefs being foisted on them by their new rulers, there were those who resisted and determined to remain loyal to the Word of God. When the troops of Antiochus entered a small village northwest of Jerusalem named Modein, demanding the villagers prove their loyalty to the king by performing a pagan sacrifice. An aged priest named Mattathias refused, and fighting broke out, resulting in the death of the king's representative. Mattathias and his five sons, Simon, John, Judas, Eleazar, and Jonathan escaped to the hills. Judas becomes known as "Maccabeus" (the hammerer), and led the revolt from 166-160 BC after Mattathias' death. In 164 Judas reclaimed the Temple, and restored religious freedom for the Jews in 162. As Judas became bolder, he began to suffer more defeats, and he was killed in 160. His brother Jonathan became the leader of the revolt at that point. He was unable to free Jerusalem from Seleucid control, but formed a truce with the Seleucid leader and in return was named high priest. Later he was given control over much of Judea and Samaria, but was murdered by one of the Seleucid leaders in 143 BC Simon, the last of Mattathias' sons, took control in 143 BC when Jonathan died. There were two contenders fighting for the Seleucid throne – Trypho and Demetrius II. Simon sided with Demetrius II in exchange for freedom for Jerusalem and Judea. In 142, this was accomplished and Simon was named high priest and ethnarch (ruler of a people). His line is called the Hasmonean Dynasty, which traces its origin back to an ancestor of Mattathias.

In 135 BC, Simon and most of his family were murdered in an attempt by Antiochus VII at a coup. However, Simon's son John Hyrcanus was not present, and therefore the coup was not successful. One of the characteristics of the Hasmonean rulers that became increasingly apparent was their attraction to the Hellenistic way of life – the very thing their forefathers had been fighting against to begin with! Although they bore the title of high priest, they were not of the lineage of the high priest, and this was an escalating problem for those who believed they should follow the law exclusively. During the reign of John Hyrcanus the sects of the Sadducees and the Pharisees developed for the first time. Ezekiel 46 states that the high priest must be chosen from the Zadokites. The Sadducees developed over this issue, but they were of the wealthier, more landed class, and were less bothered by the worldly leanings of their leader. Although John Hyrcanus did not take the title of king, he gave every appearance of being just that. He changed the names of all of his children from Hebrew names to Greek names, and employed foreign mercenaries in his army. As he conquered people, they were forced to convert to Judaism. Although most of the Jews supported him, those who were more orthodox questioned his actions. He had greater support among the Sadducees than among the Pharisees.

Upon the death of John Hyrcanus, his son Aristobulus became king – the first of the Hasmonean rulers to take that title. He imprisoned his mother and all of his brothers except one in order to prevent any rivals to the throne. Although he only reigned for one year (104-103 BC) he did conquer upper Galilee and forced the inhabitants to submit to circumcision.

When Aristobulus died in 103, his brother Alexander Jannaeus succeeded him, marrying his brother's widow in order to solidify his claim to the throne. He conquered more areas and extended the Jewish territory further than anyone else. However, there was civil war between Jannaeus and the Pharisees for six years, ending with the Pharisees appealing to King Demetrius III of Syria for help. Demetrius attacked Jannaeus and defeated him near Shechem, but the Jews rallied behind Jannaeus, and Demetrius was driven out. However, Jannaeus executed eight hundred Pharisees and their families.

In 76 BC the widow of Jannaeus, Salome Alexandra, reigned for nine years until her eldest son, Hyrcanus II assumed the position of high priest. When Salome died, her younger son, Aristobulus II tried to oust Hyrcanus II with the help of the Sadducees. Hyrcanus was the weaker of the two and would have surrendered except that an Idumean governor named Antipater (the father of Herod the Great) stepped in and rendered aid to him. Antipater was able to gain the aid of the Nabatean King Aretas III, which gave Hyrcanus II sufficient power to defeat Aristobulus.

Roman Take-Over

However, this civil war allowed Pompey to step into Jerusalem and take the city with little resistance. Jerusalem fell under Roman domination in 63 BC. Pompey annexed Syria in 64 BC and took Palestine in 63. Pompey's insertion into the Jewish Civil War helped to establish Hyrcanus as the high priest. When Pompey entered the city of Jerusalem, Hyrcanus surrendered, but Aristobulus and his supporters barricaded themselves in the Temple for three months. Pompey besieged the Temple Mount using siege dikes and ramps. Although Pompey did not damage the Temple, he offended the Jews by entering the Holy of Holies.

Although Hyrcanus was the high priest established by the Roman government, Antipater was, in reality, the unofficial power of Rome in Israel. When Antipater switched allegiance to Julius Caesar, he was rewarded by being given Roman citizenship and named "Procurator." Hyrcanus was given the title of ethnarch, which is a higher title, even though Antipater was clearly the one who wielded the authority. He immediately installed his sons, Phasael and Herod, as governors over Jerusalem and Galilee.

It was important to the Romans to establish a strong presence in Palestine due to the strength of the Parthians in Mesopotamia.

Parthia was made up of the remains of the Medo-Persian Empire, and was not conquered by Rome. Therefore, it was important to the Romans that Israel become Romanized to a certain extent – there must be enough loyalty for the country to serve as a buffer against the Parthians. However, the small Jewish state offered no economic interest to Rome, and overall was more of a nuisance. The Jews chafed under the oppression of yet another foreign rule.

With the death of Antipater, his son Herod, who had ingratiated himself to the Roman emperor, was named the king of the Jews. This was offensive to the orthodox Jews, as Herod was not even a Jew but an Idumean. To the Jews, Herod was simply symbolic of the foreigners who had not only invaded their land, but were encroaching into every area of their daily lives, trying to steal the very uniqueness of their identity as Jews. Herod

Galilee:

Galilee was an area that had a reputation for harboring bandits and insurrectionists. Flavius Josephus tells of a man named Judas the Galilean who led a rebellion against the Romans about 6 BC. He was captured and executed by Herod's sons.

After the death of Herod, his sons carried on his tradition of making themselves subservient to the Roman emperors. Herod Antipas, the tetrarch of Galilee, rebuilt the city of Sepphoris, which was about four miles from Nazareth and located on the crossroads of two main trade routes. It was a cosmopolitan Roman city that functioned as the capital of Galilee until AD 18. Antipas also honored his patron, Tiberius, by building a city on the shore of the Sea of Galilee and naming it after the emperor. Tiberius was the capital until Caligula deposed Antipas in AD 39. Although all of this building provided jobs for the people of Palestine, it also increased the taxes until the people were heavily burdened.

became known as "Herod the Great" in large part because of the building projects he undertook in his lifetime. Besides rebuilding and enlarging the Temple, which benefited the Jews, the majority of his building projects were aimed at bringing honor to his Roman patrons. He rebuilt Samaria and named it Sebaste, the Greek equivalent of Augustus. Within this city, as well as in Caesarea Maritima there was a temple dedicated to the worship of Augustus.

Besides the Roman troops in the cities, the Romans brought with them their standards emblazoned with images forbidden by Jewish laws, their games, their gymnasiums in which the young men took part in athletic competition in the nude. All of these were a constant reminder to those who strove to please God that the Romans with their paganism were a force they could not overthrow.

It is easy to see how the people hated the domination of the Romans.

CHAPTERS 1-2

Daniel bar Jamin, a Galilean youth of eighteen who has spent the last five years living with a robber band in the caves above his former village, is confronted with a dilemma when two young people his own age venture onto their mountain, and Daniel recognizes them. Overcome with a longing for contact with those from his village, as well as news concerning his grandmother and sister, Daniel approaches the two and speaks with them. The two are Joel, the son of the village rabbi, and Malthace his twin sister. Daniel asks Joel to deliver a message to Simon, who had been a blacksmith's apprentice with him. From Joel, he learns that Simon now has his own shop and is known as Simon the Zealot. Joel and his sister share their food with Daniel, and he relates to them how he came up to this area to escape his brutal master, and was discovered by Rosh, the leader of a local robber band who had been kind to him. As some Roman legionaries pass on the road below, the boys realize they share a hatred for the Roman conquerors. Daniel points out to Joel and Malthace the plain where Joshua defeated the Canaanite kings. The children speak excitedly of God sending another Deliverer, and how they thought if they came up to this place, they would be able to see Him come. Daniel offers to see the other two safely back to the road, and as they walk Joel asks if Daniel has met Rosh the outlaw. When Daniel tells him he has, Joel looks at the other boy with envy. As they are going, Daniel suddenly spies Rosh on the road. Daniel instructs Joel and Malthace to stay where they are while he goes to meet Rosh's men, discovering they are to ambush a caravan in order to seize a slave they have in their custody. Joel insists his sister hide, but he makes it plain he intends to participate in the raid on the caravan. Since it is approaching, there is no time for Daniel to argue, and Joel joins him. As the caravan comes into view, the signal is sounded, and the hills come alive with Rosh's men. As Daniel disables the man assigned to him, the others in the band free the oversized slave Rosh has requisitioned. The attack is over quickly, and their prize is recovered. Daniel notices that Joel has a bruised shoulder, and Joel explains he received the bruise from one of the mules as he tried to help Daniel. Rosh approaches and Daniel introduces Joel as a new recruit. At first Rosh tells Joel he will have to live in the caves and not return to the village, but Joel refuses, explaining he must take his sister home and go with his parents to Capernaum. Rosh consents, admonishing him to keep his eyes and ears open, and when the time comes, he will be able to be of service to him. Daniel volunteers to lead the slave, dubbed Samson, back to their camp, and spends most of the night releasing him from his shackles. As he works, he talks to him about Rosh, his fearlessness against the hated Romans, and his growing band of followers. When the man is freed, he kneels in front of Daniel, placing his forehead on Daniel's foot. He finds a cover for Samson, then lies down to sleep, the giant man at his feet.

SUGGESTED ACTIVITIES CHAPTERS 1-2

1.   Assign research into the history of Israel and particularly Galilee in relation to Rome at this period of time. If possible, have some students research from the Roman point of view, and some from the Galilean point of view, and have them report on their findings. Particularly cover the rebellion of Judas, because this is an actual historical event and Judas is a real person.

2.   Talk about the character of Rosh. Daniel and some of the more idealistic young men believe Rosh might be the Messiah promised to deliver Israel from their oppressor. Read some of the Messianic prophecies. Could Rosh fit the "resume" of the Messiah?

3.   Find pictures of the area used for the setting of the book, and show them to the students, or invite someone who has visited this area to bring in pictures or slides to show.

VOCABULARY CHAPTERS 1-2

bar	(	adj)	son of
patriotism		(n)	love of country and willingness to sacrifice for it
unreconciled		(v)	not settled or resolved
burgeoning		(adj)	growing and flourishing
cranny		(n)	a small opening, as in a wall or rock face; a crevice
scowled		(v)	to make a frowning expression of displeasure
ruddy		(adj)	of a healthy reddish complexion
flax		(n)	fiber of the flax plant that is made into thread and woven into linen fabric
tetrarch		(n)	One of four joint rulers
lured		(v)	to draw on with a promise of pleasure or gain
diverted		(v)	to turn from a course or purpose
legionaries		(n)	a unit of the Roman army comprising 3000 to 6000 soldiers
contempt		(adj)	open disrespect for a person or thing
vouch		(v)	to give a guarantee
taut		(adj)	extremely nervous; tense
treacherous		(adj)	dangerously unstable and unpredictable
lurching		(v)	walking unsteadily
dagger		(n)	a sharp pointed knife for stabbing
plagued		(adj)	a cause of annoyance; a nuisance
fracas		(n)	a noisy, disorderly fight or quarrel; a brawl
mottled		(adj)	to mark with spots of different color
indifferent		(adj)	of no importance one way or the other
livid		(adj)	discolored by bruising
wariness		(adj)	careful in guarding against danger or deception
bristling		(adj)	to be covered or thick with or as if with bristles
gnarled		(adj)	knotty or misshapen
uncomprehending		(v)	not understanding
jackals		(n)	An accomplice or a lackey who aids in the commission of base or disreputable acts
draught		(n)	a serving of drink drawn from a keg
ferocity		(adj)	the property of being wild or turbulent
manacles		(n)	a shackle for the hand or wrist
stupor		(adj)	a state of extreme apathy or torpor often following stress or shock
interminable		(adj)	tiresomely long; seemingly without end
trifle		(n)	something of little value or importance

QUESTIONS CHAPTERS 1-2

1. The setting of a story is the time and place in which it takes place. What is the setting of this story?

2. Describe Daniel.

3. Why has Daniel been living in the caves above his village? How long has he been living here?

4. Who invades his world to remind him of his previous life?

5. What family members did Daniel leave behind in the village?

6. Who else does Daniel remember as a friend?

7. What do Joel and Malthace do that Daniel has not thought about doing for five years? What emotion does he feel as he joins them in this act?

8. Who is Rosh? What did he do for Daniel five years earlier?

9. What interrupts their time together?

10. How are Joel and Daniel different? In what way are they alike?

11. What unexpected knowledge does Daniel demonstrate to Joel and Malthace?

12. Why does Daniel offer to walk part of the way with Joel and Malthace?

13. As they are walking, what does Joel confide in Daniel?

14. What conflict does Joel feel when Daniel invites him to join the band?

15. How are they interrupted?

16. What assignment is Daniel given?

17. What does Rosh tell Joel? Why does he say this? What are his final instructions to Joel?

18. How does Daniel feel after Rosh has talked to Joel?

19. As Daniel works to free the giant slave from his manacles, what does he do to pass the time?

20. Once the man is freed, what does Daniel discover about his attitude?

ANSWERS TO QUESTIONS CHAPTERS 1-2

1. The story is set in Galilee during the time of Jesus – about 30 AD.

2. Daniel is eighteen years old, tanned, tall, lean and muscular with dark eyes, black hair, and a perpetual scowl on his face.

3. He was apprenticed to a blacksmith who was abusive, and ran away to escape the abuse five years earlier.

4. The twin daughter and son of the village rabbi, Joel and Malthace, who are his age, come to the mountain for a picnic.

5. His grandmother and sister

6. There was another apprentice who worked with Daniel and was kind to him; his name was Simon. Joel tells him Simon now has his own shop, and is known as Simon the Zealot.

7. They wash their hands. He feels embarrassed – hoping none of the men who are part of the robber band he lives with will see what he is doing.

8. Rosh is the leader of a band of robbers who live in the caves above the village where Daniel used to live and where Joel and Malthace still live. Many in the village hold out hope that Rosh will lead an insurrection against the Romans because he participated in the uprising led by Judas and was able to escape. Five years earlier, he found Daniel when the boy could go no further, and carried him into the caves where he helped him to heal and made him a part of the band.

9. They see some Roman Legionaries.

10. Daniel is poor, barely educated and has lived for five years as an uncivilized heathen. Joel is from a wealthy family, is well educated and is a strict observer of the law. They both are filled with anger toward the Romans, and desire to see an army raised by Israel to overthrow their oppressors.

11. He shows them the plain where Joshua defeated the Canaanite kings, describing the battle in graphic detail.

12. He wants to make sure they are safe.

13. One of the reasons he had wanted to come up to the mountain was that he had hoped to be able to see Rosh. He tells Daniel that Rosh is the hero of all the boys at school.

14. He is torn because of his desire to follow Rosh, which conflicts with his sense of love and duty for his parents and sister.

15. One of Rosh's men shows up, blocking their way down and telling Daniel he is needed for an ambush on a caravan.

16. When the signal is given, Daniel is to jump one of the guards and disable him without killing him in order to allow the men to grab a particular slave that Rosh wants.

17. Rosh tells Joel that he will not be able to go back to the village, but will have to stay on the mountain with him. He does not want Joel to go back and talk about what he has seen. Once Joel assures him he will not talk, he tells him to go with his family to Capernaum, and await Rosh's instructions.

18. He is jealous of Rosh's attentions to Joel.

19. He talks to him about Rosh, what he is doing and what he plans to do.

20. The man virtually worships Daniel, bowing down and placing his forehead on Daniel's foot. When Daniel goes to sleep, the man sleeps at his feet.

CHAPTERS 3-4

As time passes, Daniel finds Samson both a tremendous enhancement for his work, for the large man will not leave Daniel's side; refusing to follow Rosh's orders. Rosh finally gives up and leaves him to assist Daniel with his blacksmith's work. However, the other men never overcome their fear and distrust of the large man, and Daniel finds himself included in the jokes and insults aimed at Samson. Daniel wonders if the man is truly deaf, or if he merely refuses to respond. Daniel believes Samson is capable of understanding more than the others give him credit for, and he wonders what goes on in the large man's mind. As they take a break from the forge to eat one afternoon, Rosh calls Daniel and he finds there is a stranger in the camp who has been brought in blindfolded. Daniel is delighted to see his friend Simon, who has received his message from Joel. Daniel shows Simon his forge, demonstrating the weapons he makes for Rosh and company. Simon delivers the reason for his visit – Daniel's old master, Amakek, is dead, and he feels Daniel might want to return to the village for the sake of his grandmother and sister. Although Daniel has little desire to see them, Simon talks him into coming down for a day or two in order to let them see he is all right. As he starts down the mountain with Simon, Daniel is taken off guard by Samson trying to follow him. He manages to make the man understand he cannot go with him and continues with Simon. As they walk Daniel discovers that Simon does not approve of Rosh's methods, even though he is a Zealot and opposes the Roman oppressors. When they come to a stream, Simon suggests they go ahead and bathe because it will be too late when they reach the village – the Sabbath will have begun. Daniel is embarrassed to realize he has no idea what day it is. He no longer observes the Sabbath. When Daniel reaches his previous home, he finds it crumbling in disrepair. His grandmother is waiting for him

and is delighted to see him. His blond sister, who trembles with fear, does not recognize him at first and shies away from him. He is disappointed at seeing the fear still in his sister's eyes. As the last call of the horn announcing the beginning of the Sabbath sounds, his grandmother asks Daniel to speak the words of the blessing for the Sabbath. Stumbling over them at first, Daniel finds they come back to him as he recites them. There is little food, and neither his grandmother nor his sister is eating. His grandmother says they have already eaten, but his sister informs him they have saved their food for him. As they prepare for bed, Daniel is thankful to escape to the roof where he is overcome with homesickness for his cave.

The next morning, Simon shows up and invites Daniel to accompany him to synagogue. He is reluctant at first, but Simon has brought some of his own old clothes for Daniel to wear, and tells him there is a visiting preacher he wants Daniel to hear. Daniel knows that if Simon has broken the law by carrying the bundle of clothes to him on the Sabbath, it must be very important to him for Daniel to see this man, and decides to go with him. When Simon asks how it is for Daniel to be home, Daniel blurts out that his grandmother sleeps all the time and his sister is possessed by demons – it can hardly be called home. Simon explains the man they are going to hear is Jesus of Nazareth, who preaches the coming of the kingdom. Daniel is surprised at the number of people present at the synagogue. The interest in Jesus has drawn a crowd like Daniel has never seen before. As Jesus stands to speak, Daniel feels his spirit stirring within him. However, he is confused when Jesus speaks of repentance rather than raising an army to fight against the oppressors. After they leave, Simon tells him of an incident that occurred in Nazareth in which the people of the village tried to stone Jesus and He managed to walk away from them.

Daniel is disappointed that Jesus did not fight His way through the crowd. He asks Simon what Jesus meant when He said the day is at hand for the kingdom of God, but Simon cannot explain. As they part ways, Simon promises to look in on him the next day. Daniel takes his time as he makes his way to his grandmother's house. The peace is suddenly shattered by a detachment of Roman cavalry passing through the village. Daniel's anger is roused. He picks up a rock and shouts "Infidels" at the soldiers. He is quickly grabbed by two men from the village, who cover his mouth and hold him back. When they ask his name, they respond he should know better. They ask if he wants to bring down the same curse on all of them. He tells them he has taken an oath, but they warn him to keep it to himself or the entire village will be burned to the ground like Sepphoris. Daniel knows he has acted foolishly and he cannot abide staying confined in the stifling streets of the village. He takes off for the mountain after dark. When he arrives, he finds Samson waiting where he left him.

SUGGESTED ACTIVITIES CHAPTERS 3-4

1.   Assign research on the Zealots: who were they; how did they begin; what did they believe, etc.

2.   Leah works with a loom. Arrange a visit so students can see how a loom works and the cloth that is produced from the loom.

3.   Have students make maps of Israel with particular attention to Galilee and the area involved in the story.

4.   Have students illustrate characters from the book.

VOCABULARY CHAPTERS 3-4

baffled	(adj)	perplexed by many conflicting situations or statements
jibes	(n)	taunting, heckling, or jeering remarks
impassive	(adj)	showing no signs of feeling, emotion, or interest
pilfered	(v)	to steal in small quantities
affably	(adv)	courteous and agreeable in conversation
chagrined	(adj)	feeling or caused to feel uneasy and self-conscious
Torah	(n)	the whole body of the Jewish sacred writings and tradition including the oral tradition
tallith	(n)	a shawl with a ritually knotted fringe at each corner; worn by Jews at morning prayer

QUESTIONS CHAPTERS 3-4

1. In what ways has Samson proven to be a help to Daniel?

2. How does Rosh feel about Samson?

3. Read Exodus 20:15 and Proverbs 10:2. How do these verses apply to the manner in which Rosh obtained Samson and the resulting consequences in the way Rosh felt?

4. What is Samson's relationship to Daniel? How does it affect the way the other men treat Daniel?

5. Who comes to the camp to visit Daniel? Why does he come?

6. What conflict does Daniel feel when Simon asks if he doesn't want to see his grandmother and sister?

7. What unexpected problem arises when Daniel starts down the mountain?

8. As Daniel and Simon talk of Rosh, and Simon says he and Rosh do not see eye to eye, what is the example he gives of one way they are different?

9. What does Simon remind Daniel of that he has forgotten?

10. What emotion does Daniel feel as he goes to bed in his old place on the roof that night?

11. What does Simon tell him the next morning?

12. How does Daniel feel when he first sees Jesus?

13. What does Jesus say that Daniel finds unsettling?

14. What happens to Daniel on his way home?

15. Write a journal entry as if you are Daniel, telling about this part of the story.

ANSWERS TO QUESTIONS CHAPTERS 3-4

1. Because he is large and powerful, Samson is able to work the bellows for Daniel's smelting oven tirelessly. He also seems impervious to the heat, appearing to have come from a place where such heat is common. Samson also keeps the camp supplied with firewood and helps with any chores which require more muscle than the other men are able to supply.

2. Rosh is disgusted because the man has never come to see Rosh as his master. He will not follow Rosh's orders, and continues to follow Daniel around, giving only Daniel his complete loyalty.

3. Scripture admonishes us not to steal, and Samson was stolen from a caravan. Proverbs 10:2 states that "ill-gotten gains do not profit," and this is certainly true in the case of Samson and Rosh. Rosh had his eye on this slave in the same way that someone would pick out a new car or a new outfit of clothing in advance, planning for its purchase and desiring it. However, he did not obtain him in a lawful way, but stole that which belonged to someone else. (Of course, this is a man and not merchandise, but we will not go into the morality of slavery here). All of this leaves Rosh with the taste of sawdust in his mouth.

4. Samson feels gratitude toward Daniel who not only freed him from his shackles, but also talked to him as a human being and refused to treat him in the same demeaning way the others have. Samson is totally and completely loyal to Daniel and will not leave his side. To Daniel's chagrin, this causes the other men to include him in the insults they lob against Samson.

5. Simon the Zealot comes to visit Daniel because he has received Daniel's message from Joel, and wants to let him know that Amalek, his former master, has died.

6. Daniel realizes he does not want to see his grandmother and sister, although he knows he should want to. This leaves him feeling guilty and embarrassed.

7. Samson tries to go with him, and he has to make him understand he cannot accompany him down the mountain and into the village.

8. Simon tells Daniel that he believes in earning the money for his food, although Rosh steals what he wants from the neighboring farmers.

9. It is the beginning of the Sabbath, and they need to wash before it begins.

10. He is homesick for his companions in the mountains.

11. Simon wants him to accompany him to the synagogue, as there is a man there who is preaching that Simon thinks he should hear.

12. Daniel's spirit is stirred, and he feels excited and electrified.

13. Rather than talking about raising an army and fighting against the Romans, Jesus says they should "Repent and believe."

14. A detachment of Roman cavalry passes through the village, and Daniel shouts out "Infidel" at them and tries to throw a rock, but is stopped by some of the villagers.

15. Answers will vary.

CHAPTERS 5-6

As the time of harvest progresses in the fields below the mountains, Daniel's desire to see the Romans driven from the land becomes increasingly urgent. Driven by the need to find someone else with his same dreams and ambitions, he searches the trails around the village for Joel, even though he knows the other boy has moved to Capernaum. Finally hatching a plan that will allow him to reach Joel once again, he goes to Rosh and seeks permission to go to the city and seek out the rabbi's son. Although Rosh is doubtful of Joel's true allegiance to his cause, he gives Daniel his head and sends him on his way. Daniel reaches the city too early to look for Joel, and decides to take in the sites of the city. He wanders about, taking in all that he can of the marketplace with its variety of colors, sounds and smells. When he sees a black slave similar to Samson, he wonders if the man would be able to understand Samson's language. Coming to the harbor, he finds the fishing boats moored and a crowd gathered. A young woman offers him something to eat, and asks if he is waiting to hear the teacher. He asks what teacher, and is told it is the carpenter who is coming now. As Daniel listens to Jesus for the second time, he feels his own spirit excited as it was in the synagogue. Two soldiers distract him, and Daniel spits, bringing contemptuous looks from the men. Jesus ignores them and continues speaking. Daniel has heard enough and turns to leave. He is amazed at the symbiotic relationship he sees between the Romans and the Jews in the city. When Daniel is directed to the home of Rabbi Hezron,, Daniel has counted on Joel observing the law by providing him with food and shelter, but he begins to have doubts when he realizes the immensity of the family's wealth. Announcing his presence at the gate and asking to see Joel, he is greeted instead by Malthace. Her greeting is somewhat cool, but Joel emerges and greets Daniel warmly, inviting him to stay to eat. Joel leads Daniel to his room and pumps him for information. When they go to dinner, it is obvious to Daniel he is not welcomed by Joel's father. Hezron questions Daniel about his home, his family and his background, sparking several angry memories in the boy. Hezron dismisses

Daniel's father as a "good man, but a rash one," then asks Daniel if he is following his father's trade. Daniel replies that he was bound to Amalek, the ironsmith. Inwardly Daniel seethes that he was sold into slavery to a cruel man while not even the rabbi protested. As the conversation continues, Daniel's ire becomes more vociferous as Hezron speaks of the things the Romans have done for the Jews in Capernaum. The meal ends with Hezron admonishing Daniel to leave and not return, sending a servant with him to make sure he gets started on the right road. Daniel is devastated, feeling he has failed Rosh in this mission, and Rosh will never trust him again. Even more bitter is the disappointment of losing the only friend he has ever had.

As Daniel begins on his way, he is accosted by a Roman soldier who demands the boy water his horse. Rationalizing that the horse is as much a slave in the hands of the Romans as he, he decides he can water the horse, and does so. The soldier then demands water for himself. Daniel holds the same bowl up to the man, who kicks at Daniel, missing his mark. Daniel flings the water in the man's face, enraging the soldier. Daniel feels a blow to his ribs, then begins to run. He hides in a garden terrace, gathering his wits and trying to determine where he might go to escape. Realizing he is losing his grasp on consciousness, he makes his way to the only place he knows to go for help – back to Joel. He does not even remember how he made it to the door, but once there he requests the doorman call Joel. Instead, Malthace appears, urging him to depart. As she tells him Joel's studies are more important than anything else, Daniel seems unable to comprehend. He loses consciousness and awakens in a storage room. She brings him some wine and dresses his wound, then returns later with Joel. Joel informs him he knows what happened; they are searching everywhere for him. The brother and sister drag him into a passage between the walls where he will not be discovered. As Daniel drifts off to sleep, he believes he hears his mother wishing him a good night.

SUGGESTED ACTIVITIES CHAPTERS 5-6

1. Have a discussion about Daniel's perception of the Messiah. Why does he (as well as most of the Israelites of that time) see the Messiah only as a military deliverer? Is this different from people today who only call on Jesus when circumstances in their lives are bad and they need deliverance from the bad things that are happening?

2. Have students illustrate or make a model of Joel and Malthace's home in Capernaum.

3. Have one student act as a reporter interviewing the Roman soldier and any witnesses to the incident involving Daniel and the water. Assign the parts of the soldier and bystanders to members of the class. See who can come up with the most creative details without corrupting the storyline.

VOCABULARY CHAPTERS 5-6

outlandish	(adj)	conspicuously or grossly unconventional or unusual
phylacteries	(n)	one of two small square leather boxes containing slips inscribed with scripture passages and traditionally worn on the left arm and forehead by Jewish men
tantalizing	(adj)	arousing desire or expectation for something unattainable or mockingly out of reach
cohort	(n)	One of the 10 divisions of a Roman legion, consisting of 300 to 600 men
impudent	(adj)	contemptuous boldness or disregard of others

QUESTIONS CHAPTERS 5-6

1. What time of year is it?

2. How is Daniel feeling?

3. What plan does he devise and present to Rosh?

4. How does Rosh react?

5. When Daniel reaches Capernaum, Whom does he encounter for the second time? What effect does this have on him?

6. What happens to distract Daniel from the message? What are the results of this?

7. When he finds Joel's home, what about the house surprises him? What doubts does this cause him to have?

8. How is Joel's welcome different from his sister's?

9. How does Joel's father receive Daniel?

10. What does Daniel do at the dinner table that escalates into a serious problem?

11. How does Joel's father respond?

12. What is Daniel's reaction?

13. What does Daniel do that leads him into deeper trouble?

14. Where does he go for help?

15. What does Malthace tell him?

16. What does she do for Daniel?

17. Where do they hide him?

18. What does Joel tell Daniel about his father?

19. What is the last thing Daniel thinks he hears?

20. Write a journal entry as if you are Joel or Malthace, telling about what has happened from their perspective.

ANSWERS TO QUESTIONS CHAPTERS 5-6

1. It is springtime; the time of harvest for the fields of barley.

2. Daniel is restless, ready to go to war against the Romans and impatient with merely waiting and raiding caravans with Rosh.

3. As a desire arises in him to see Joel again, Daniel concocts a plan to go to Capernaum and seek Joel out and give him another chance to join Rosh' band.

4. Rosh does not encourage him, telling him Joel's grandfather is very wealthy and Joel is not likely to give it all up in order to join them. He tells him to go ahead, anyway; adding that Joel might be of use to them in the city.

5. Daniel has a second encounter with Jesus and his spirit is stirred within him, just as it was the first time he heard Jesus speak.

6. Two Roman soldiers join the crowd just behind Daniel, causing his anger to rise. When he spits to show his disgust at this development, the fishermen are more disturbed at him than at the Romans. He is even more perplexed at Jesus, who takes no notice of the soldiers at all.

7. Daniel was not prepared for the level of wealth Joel's family possesses. He begins to doubt whether or not they will feel constrained to follow the requirements of the law concerning providing food and shelter to strangers at one's door.

8. Malthace is obviously distraught at seeing him, shrinking back from him and treating him coldly even after Joel has arrived. Joel, on the other hand, is genuinely thrilled to see him and greets him warmly and affectionately.

9. Hezron receives Daniel coolly, noticing his poor clothing and even poorer manners.

10. Daniel speaks his mind about all of the Roman influence he has seen in Capernaum, particularly in regard to the Jewish temple built with Roman funds.

11. He has Joel removed from the house, telling him he is never to return.

12. Daniel is left on the road in a pool of self-pity, humiliation and despair. He berates himself for totally bungling his mission, and feels he has let Rosh down as well as losing Joel, the only friend he has ever had.

13. After leaving Joel's house, he is stopped by a Roman soldier ordering Daniel to give water to his horse. After Daniel waters the horse, the soldier demands water for himself and Daniel holds up the same bowl. When the man angrily demands clean water, giving him a kick, Daniel throws water into the soldier's face. This results in Daniel being stabbed in the side.

14. The only place he knows to go is to Joel's house.

15. At first she tells him to go away; he should not be distracted from his studies, and if Daniel cared anything about Joel he would leave him alone so that he could complete his studies and become a famous rabbi. Until Daniel faints, she does not realize he is injured.

16. She drags him into a storage room to hide him, gives him wine with medication in it and dresses his wound.

17. There is a passage between the walls in the storage room, and they drag him there.

18. Joel says his father has suspected the way he feels, and fears Joel will join the Zealots.

19. He thinks he hears his mother saying, "Goodnight, Daniel."

20. Answers will vary.

CHAPTERS 7-8

As Daniel recuperates, Joel reads to him from the Scripture and Daniel tries to store the words in his memory in order to sustain him as he returns to the mountain. The three young people sit together discussing what Joel has read; mulling over the prophecies and trying to determine if Rosh might be the one they are speaking of. Thacia points out it is not likely that Rosh, an outlaw, would be the one to fulfill the prophecies. The two young men argue with her that it does not matter what kind of man brings in the kingdom, as long as the Romans are defeated. As Daniel becomes more impassioned, he begins to relate to them the story of how his parents were killed by the Romans, leading him to take a vow at the age of eight to avenge them. Daniel's uncle, arrested for not paying his taxes, had tried to fight against the Romans and was told he would be taken to the quarries to work off his debt. Daniel's father, along with four others from the village had lain in wait in a cornfield and ambushed the soldiers as they transferred the prisoner. All the men were crucified. Daniel's mother, overcome with grief, had stayed at the crosses for two days and had come home sick, only to die a few weeks later. His five-year-old sister had also come to the crosses and had been tormented with terrible nightmares after that. She would not leave the house, and was believed to be demon possessed. Moved by his story, Joel swears a vow against the Romans also. Thacia then joins in, declaring that if Deborah and Queen Esther could serve Israel, she could also take a vow to fight for Israel. At first Daniel says no, it is not for "a pretty child." He acquiesces when Joel declares they will all three swear a new vow – the three of them together. They swear a vow "For God's Victory." Joel declares he will go back to the mountain with Daniel when he is healed, but Daniel tells him Rosh wants Joel where he is. He tells him Rosh has something in mind for Joel, but he does not know what it is. Devising a signal to know when Daniel returns with word from Rosh, Thacia suggests the bronze bow from David's song they had read in the Scripture (2 Samuel 22:35). Thacia promises she will play her harp for him after the Sabbath, and the brother and sister leave. This time he hears her wishing him goodnight. After they are gone, Daniel decides it will be best for him to slip out without the others knowing, and leaves early the next morning – on the Sabbath – while the others are still asleep.

On the path, Daniel realizes he has left the shelter of Joel's house too soon. He is still weak, and is faint by the time he reaches the foot of the mountain. Samson bounds down the side of the mountain and carries him up, not allowing him on his feet again for three days. The men in the cave have heard of Daniel's experience in Capernaum, giving him up for dead. After a brief period in which he is held to be a hero by the men, life returns to normal with the exception of Daniel's inner life. Daniel cannot forget his time with Joel and Thacia, and longs for the time when he can see Joel again. His opportunity arrives when Rosh demands he repair a dagger that has carried particular significance for him and that has become entirely mangled. Daniel explains it will need a rivet; he does not have the capacity to repair the dagger, but might be able to take it to Simon in the village. Daniel feels uneasy, realizing Rosh expects him to simply take what is needed from Simon; he has given Daniel no money. When Daniel reaches the village, he finds the blacksmith shop closed up, and is informed Simon has followed after a preacher and has been gone for a month. Daniel knows he cannot return to Rosh empty-handed, and refuses to break into Simon's shop. He heads to Capernaum believing the Roman soldier will not recognize him there after time has passed. He also realizes he has been looking for an excuse to go to Capernaum. Reaching the city, he inquires about the whereabouts of Jesus and is told He is in Behsaida. Daniel makes his way to Joel's house and secrets himself in the passageway, awaiting Joel. Joel finally discovers him and he explains his errand. Joel tells Daniel his father has said Jesus is dangerous, but he would like to find out for himself what He is like. As they go, they meet a family with a young son bitten by a camel on their way to ask Jesus to heal the boy's hand. Puzzled, Daniel asks if He is a doctor as well, and the man asks where he is from that he does not know about the preacher and how He has healed people. Finding the house of Simon Peter, they push through the crowd until Daniel is able to catch the attention of Simon the Zealot. Simon introduces Daniel to Jesus, and he again feels the disturbance in his spirit. As they sit down to eat, the question is posed to Jesus as to why the members of the household do not observe the Law, since there was not water provided for all to wash their hands. Jesus replies that they should prepare their hearts rather than their hands to receive the gift, then blesses the food. Daniel watches as Joel takes a bite of food; probably deliberately breaking the Law for the first time in his life. When the meal is over, the clamor begins for those who are sick to be healed. Among those healed is the boy Daniel and Joel had seen on their way. Daniel finds Simon again, asking how this can be possible, and Simon replies he does not understand it, but Jesus is able to heal, although he does not understand why all are not healed. Jesus speaks, and Daniel feels the same stirring in his spirit he has felt before. Jesus talks of the kingdom and Daniel wonders how this can apply to those gathered at this place now – the poor, lame, and blind. Jesus appears to become weary, and His disciples take him into the house. Daniel explains his errand to Simon, who tells him of a blacksmith in the city where he has been working sometimes. He says the man owes him wages, and Daniel can have what he needs in exchange for Simon's wages. Daniel asks if he won't need them, and Simon replies he does not. Daniel asks if he has come to ask Jesus to join the Zealots, but Simon tells him it has not turned out that way. Now he is hoping to join Jesus. As they leave, Joel confides that he believes his father is right. Jesus is dangerous and is not a true rabbi.

SUGGESTED ACTIVITIES CHAPTERS 7-8

1. Visit a museum, particularly an interactive one, where students will be able to see a blacksmith at work in order to see the kind of work Daniel is doing. An interactive museum where they are able to try some of the work would be best.

2. If arrangements can be made, have students minister to residents in a nursing home or children in the hospital, just as Joel and Malthace ministered to Daniel in the story. If visiting children in the hospital, they could prepare a basket for each child with items to be used by the child in the hospital – coloring books and crayons, crossword puzzle books for older children, small games that can be played alone, etc.

3. Have students make a poster with 2 Samuel 22:34-36 written on it and an illustration showing the bronze bow with a visual depiction of their concept of the interpretation of these verses.

VOCABULARY CHAPTERS 7-8

immensity	(adj)	very great in size or degree
quarries	(n)	a surface excavation for extracting stone or slate
avenge	(v)	to inflict a punishment or penalty in return for a wrong; revenge
toiling	(v)	to proceed with great effort
disputed	(v)	to deny the truth or rightness of
exploit	(n)	a notable or heroic act
talisman	(n)	an object thought to act as a charm
chasm	(n)	a deep opening in the earth's surface
reproach	(n)	an expression of disapproval
clamor	(n)	a loud continuous noise
frenzy	(n)	a state of violent mental agitation or wild excitement

QUESTIONS CHAPTERS 7-8

1. As Daniel is healing, what does Joel to help pass the time?

2. What is the effect this has on Daniel? What does this say about the Word of God?

3. How much time has passed since Daniel first came back to Joel's house?

4. What does Joel say about Rosh?

5. What does Thacia point out?

6. What does Daniel reveal about his parents? How has this shaped his present emotional state?

7. After Daniel has confided in Joel and Thacia his history, what decision is made?

8. What does Joel say he will do when Daniel is ready to leave? What does Daniel tell him Rosh wants him to do?

9. Where do they get the idea of the bronze bow?

10. What explanation does Thacia give for the meaning of the bronze bow? How does Joel respond?

11. What does Daniel decide he has to do? Why? When does he do it?

12. What is Daniel's attitude toward the Law?

13. What does Daniel discover as he walks toward the mountain? How does he make it up the trail?

14. In what way has his stature among the men at the cave changed since he left to go to Capernaum?

15. How has Daniel changed since his trip to Capernaum?

16. What happens that gives him an opportunity to make another visit to the city?

17. What does he discover when he goes to Simon's shop? Where is he told Simon has gone?

18. What does Joel tell him his father has said about Jesus?

19. What does Jesus do that stirs up the Jews who were strictest about following the ceremonial laws?

20. Write two paragraphs about the experience of the boys with Jesus: one from the perspective of Daniel and one from the perspective of Joel.

ANSWERS TO QUESTIONS CHAPTERS 7-8

1. Joel reads to Daniel and Malthace from the Scripture.

2. The words worked on Daniel's soul "like the wine that Thacia brought him every evening." He tries to store them up in his heart so he will be able to carry them with him when he returns to themountain. The Word of God is a consuming fire (Jeremiah 5:14); a life-giving force (Ezekial 37:7); a saving power (Romans 1:16); a piercing instrument (Hebrews 4:12); and food for the soul (1 Peter 2:2).

3. 5 days

4. Joel asks if Daniel thinks Rosh could be the one they are looking for who will deliver them from the Romans – the Messiah.

5. She says it is unlikely that God will use an outlaw to bring his Kingdom into being.

6. Daniel relates how his parents died as a result of his father attacking a group of Roman soldiers in an attempt to free his uncle, who was a prisoner. Both his father and uncle were crucified, and his mother stayed at the cross for two days and nights, returning home ill and dying within a few weeks. It was his parents' deaths that caused Daniel to hate the Romans and to take an oath to avenge their deaths by fighting against the Romans in any way he can.

7. Both Joel and Thacia take an oath as well, that they will fight for God's victory against the Romans.

8. Joel tells Daniel he will quit his studies and go back with him to the mountain, but Daniel replies that Rosh wants Joel to stay where he is to be useful to Rosh within the city of Capernaum.

9. They take the idea from David's song in 2 Samuel 22:35.

10. She says that it is a bow that can't be bent by a man alone, but that God strengthens us to do things that seem to be impossible. Joel dismisses her explanation as that of a highly active imagination.

11. Daniel decides it is time for him to leave, and goes while the family is asleep because he does not want Joel to protest and try to keep him there.

12. Daniel believes the Law applies only to the wealthy and the scholars, not to the poor.

13. He should have waited longer before leaving Joel's house. He is weaker than he thought, and nearly faints as he comes close to the foot of the mountain.

14. News of what happened to him in Capernaum has reached the cave before him, and the men treat him as a hero – at least for a while.

15. In Joel he has found a true friend, one who shares his goals and desires in life, and he has been able to confide in him and share things with him that he has never been able to do with anyone before. He finds his mind dwelling constantly on Joel and what happened while he was with him, while his heart yearns to be with Joel again.

16. Rosh breaks a dagger that is particularly important to him and demands Daniel to fix it. However, Daniel does not have the parts or the capacity to fix it on the mountain, and suggests going to Simon's shop in order to get what he needs.

17. Simon's shop is closed up, and he is told Simon has gone to follow a preacher. He has been gone for about a month.

18. His father has said Jesus is dangerous; He is not a true rabbi; it's dangerous to even listen to Him.

19. When the people in the house eat without washing their hands, He is asked why they do not observe the Law. He responds that it is more important to cleanse their hearts than to cleanse their hands.

20. Answers will vary.

CHAPTERS 9-11

Five days after Daniel returns from his journey to Capernaum to repair Rosh's dagger, Rosh sends him on his first solo assignment. Daniel is anxious, desiring to prove himself worthy to Rosh and not fail this test. Rosh has instructed him that the old man he is looking for lives like a pauper, but is in truth very wealthy, and travels across the mountains once a month carrying a bag of gold while pretending to be a beggar. According to Rosh, he is smuggling money to a friend who is buying property for him in Antioch, and one day he will just disappear for good. Before he does, Rosh intends to take what he considers to be his part of the man's gold. Daniel lies in wait as ordered, and takes the man easily, but as he walks away from the old man lying in the road, is reminded of his aged grandfather, and is unable to leave the man to die in the road. He carries him to the side of the road and waits until he regains consciousness, only returning to Rosh after the man has tottered away. When Daniel returns to camp, Rosh is aware of what has happened, and derides him for having a soft spot. Daniel tells Rosh he is after Roman blood; he does not understand why they have to fight against other Jews. Rosh tells him he has a weakness in him that has to be hammered out, just as Daniel would hammer out a bubble in his ironworks. As Daniel works, he thinks about what Rosh has said, and believes he is right. However, he feels there may be something wrong in Rosh's argument, and tries to think what it might be. As he thinks, he remembers the words of Jesus, and realizes that while Rosh sees a man as something to be used, Jesus sees each man as a child of God. As Daniel works and broods, Samson watches him.

In August Daniel receives a message written on a piece of broken pottery sent from Simon telling him his grandmother is dying. Ebol, the sentry, has had the message for three days, and Daniel carries it for another day before making the decision to go to the village. When he arrives at his grandmother's house, he finds the door locked. The neighbors tell him his grandmother and sister have been locked inside for a week, and they do not know if the old woman is alive or dead. Daniel asks why someone has not broken down the door, and they reply the girl is possessed with demons and will allow no one near her. One of the neighbors tells him they have tossed bread in through the window, but will come no closer than that. Daniel calls out to Leah that it is her brother, but there is no response from within the house. Daniel finally breaks down the door to find his grandmother lying on a pallet of straw and Leah crouching over her. His grandmother speaks to him, and Daniel sends one of the neighbors for the doctor. The doctor tells him his grandmother has only been hanging on to life by willpower, waiting for him to come. He instructs Daniel to look after his sister instead and see that she eats. As he sits with his grandmother that night, he begins to talk to her as he did to Samson the first night he was on the mountain. He speaks of the memories he has of her and the stories she told them as children, reciting the Twenty-third Psalm to her. As he talks, he feels his grandmother relaxing, and Leah silently creeps over to him and places her hand in his. Sometime in the night, his grandmother stops breathing and passes into eternity.

The burial of Daniel's grandmother takes place the next morning, with only a few neighbor women to mourn along with Daniel. As Daniel returns home, he is met by Simon, who has hurried to the village to try to attend the funeral, but is too late. Simon proposes Daniel take over his shop, since he has become a follower of Jesus and the shop is sitting idle. When Daniel protests, Simon tells him the farmers need someone to mend their plows and he needs someone to look after the shop. Daniel feels trapped; it seems everyone is making plans for his life. Still, he knows Leah cannot be left alone. He brings up this subject to Simon. How can he leave Leah during the day while he works? Simon suggests Daniel and Leah move into his house, which is connected to the shop, and he will be able to keep an eye on Leah while he works. Daniel is touched and thanks Simon, who dismisses his kindness as merely good business. There is one constraint he asks from Daniel. Daniel is to provide service to any Roman legionary who enters the shop needing work. At first, Daniel defiantly refuses, but

Simon explains that any rash actions would bring down the wrath of Rome not only on Daniel, but also on other members of the village. Daniel makes a trip up the mountain to inform Rosh of his intentions, and Rosh reiterates his evaluation of Daniel as soft. Daniel tells Rosh he will prove him wrong. As Daniel tries to prepare Leah to move from one dwelling to another, he faces her reluctance to leave her home. Finally neighbors come up with a solution when one of the women sews cloaks together to form curtains surrounding a box on a litter, and the men come to the door, telling Daniel they will remain out of sight until he is able to coax Leah into the litter. Speaking to her about the Queen of Sheba and Queen Esther, he is able to pique her curiosity sufficiently to draw her into the litter and move her to their new home. The men of the village soon find Daniel an able blacksmith, and he does not lack for work to keep him busy. For the first time in his life, he is able to earn money and buy food with the money he earns. He tries to encourage Leah to work at her loom, but Leah does not know where her grandmother bought the thread for the loom. Daniel has assumed Leah's weaving has been bought by sympathetic neighbors, but he is surprised one day when the servant of a wealthy woman in Chorazin comes to the shop with skeins of fine linen for Leah. Daniel learns the wealthy woman has been buying her cloth for its fine quality. Discovering some wheat flour on Simon's shelf one day, Daniel decides to try making bread, but is corrected by Leah who takes over the process and shows him how it is done. He also discovers Simon had a vegetable garden behind the house, and some vegetables begin to come up among the weeds. Leah points out to him which plants are vegetables and which are weeds, expertly working among the plants. Although he is encouraged at Leah's progress, he finds she is easily tired and very fretful, and she complains of the men who come to the shop. When a Roman soldier appears at his shop late one afternoon with a broken bridle ring, Daniel almost forgets what Simon has made him promise. As he waits for Daniel to finish, the soldier pulls off his helmet, and Daniel sees he is very young – no older than Joel, with blond hair and blue eyes. Daniel sees the young man's eyes turned toward the door to the house, which has been left open. Leah is coming through the door from the garden. Daniel lunges, slamming the door, but not before the soldier sees Leah and the rage boils within Daniel. That night he thinks of the mountain.

SUGGESTED ACTIVITIES CHAPTERS 9-11

1. Prepare a litter like the one used to transport Leah, and have female students act as Leah while others transport her.

2. Have students bake bread and/or grow a vegetable garden like Daniel and Leah have done.

3. Ask students to illustrate the Roman soldier who comes into Daniel's shop at the end of Chapter 11.

VOCABULARY CHAPTERS 9-11

sullenly	(adv)	gloomily silent
fetid	(adj)	having an offensive smell; stinking
disheveled	(adj)	in disarray; extremely disorderly
despair	(n)	utter loss of hope
dominion	(n)	control or the exercise of control
trundling	(v)	rolling
shackles	(n)	a restraint that confines or restricts freedom
salvage	(v)	to rescue from destruction
inveigled	(v)	to win over by flattery; entice
piqued	(v)	to provoke; arouse
suspicion	(n)	a state of uncertainty; doubt
plundering	(v)	to take the goods of by force or wrongfully
trivial	(adj)	of little importance
shuttle	(n)	an instrument used in weaving for passing the horizontal threads between the vertical threads

QUESTIONS CHAPTERS 9-11

1. What has Rosh given Daniel as his first "solo" assignment?

2. In what way does the man surprise Daniel?

3. What image comes into Daniel's mind as he starts to walk away from the man? What does he decide to do?

4. As a consequence of his actions, what does Rosh say about Daniel?

5. A simile is a comparison using "like" or "as." What simile is used to describe what Rosh defines as a soft spot in Daniel?

6. A metaphor is a comparison which does not use "like" or "as." What is the metaphor used in the same passage?

7. As Daniel considers Rosh's words, whose words come to his mind? How are the different?

8. What message is brought to Daniel? Who sent the message?

9. What does he find at his grandmother's house? Why won't the neighbors enter the house?

10. How does Daniel enter the house?

11. What does the doctor tell Daniel?

12. When the neighbors bring oil to him, what does Daniel realize he has forgotten about the village?

13. How does Daniel minister to his grandmother during her last night of life? In what way does this also minister to Leah?

14. Who comes after Daniel's grandmother's funeral?

15. What does Simon offer Daniel?

16. How does Daniel feel?

17. What is Rosh's reaction to Daniel's plan?

18. How does Leah react to their departure? What suggestion does one of the neighbor men make? What solution is finally reached to accommodate Leah's fears?

19. To whom does Daniel compare Leah?

20. What problem does Daniel have in trying to get Leah to start weaving on her loom again? How is this solved?

21. What does Daniel discover when he tries to bake a loaf of bread?

22. What discovery does Daniel make behind the house? How is Leah helpful in this?

23. Just as Daniel becomes encouraged about Leah's progress, what does he learn? How does he deal with this?

24. Who comes into Daniel's shop that causes a severe test for Daniel and the promise he has made to Simon?

25. What happens that causes Daniel to become severely angry? What is his first thought?

ANSWERS TO QUESTIONS CHAPTERS 9-11

1. He is to attack an old man Rosh has identified as a wealthy old miser who lives like a pauper, pretending to be a beggar as he travels through the hills carrying his wealth out of Galilee. Daniel is to ambush the man and steal the bag of money he has concealed in his girdle – Rosh considers it the man's "contribution" to the cause.

2. Because the man is old and frail, Daniel is surprised at his strength when he tries to fight back and defend himself.

3. As Daniel sees the old man lying helpless on the road, he remembers his old grandfather as he had seen him early in the morning during his childhood. Instead of leaving the man on the road, Daniel drags the man into a shaded area until he regains consciousness, then sets him on his feet and returns one of his daggers to him before he goes on his way.

4. Rosh tells him he has a soft streak in him.

5. Rosh says it is "like a bad streak in a piece of metal."

6. Rosh tells him he has to "hammer it out the way you'd hammer out a bubble"

7. Daniel remembers the words of Jesus, and realizes that Rosh only sees men as tools to be used, whereas Jesus sees each person as a child of God.

8. Daniel receives a message that his grandmother is dying. It has been sent by Simon the Zealot.

9. When he arrives at his grandmother's house, the door is locked and some of the neighbors are gathered on the outside, but no one will go in. The neighbors are afraid because it is believed that his sister is demon possessed.

10. He breaks down the door.

11. He tells him to look after his sister and make sure she gets something to eat – his grandmother has been hanging on by sheer willpower, waiting for him to come. Now he needs to let her go.

12. He talks to her through the night, just as he talked to Samson. He talks of the memories he has of the stories she told them when they were children, and he recites the twenty-third Psalm to her, as it was her favorite.

13. His words also minister calmness to Leah, and she creeps closer to him, placing her hand in his.

14. Simon

15. Simon tells Daniel he can take over the blacksmith shop in town – Simon's old shop, since he has become a follower of Jesus. He makes it sound like Daniel would be doing him a favor. He also offers to allow Daniel to live in his house, which is connected to the shop.

16. Daniel feels he is trapped, shackled to Leah.

17. Rosh tells him again he is soft, advising him to turn Leah over to the elders of the town to be cared for through the charity of the synagogue.

18. Leah is terrified of leaving the house. When the door is opened, she shrinks back from the outside in fear, and refuses to budge. One of the neighbors suggests tying her up, but Daniel cannot bring himself to think of doing that. They finally manage to move her by producing a litter in which she will be fully concealed while four men transport her across town.

19. Samson

20. He does not know where to obtain the thread she uses to weave the cloth, and neither does Leah; their grandmother has always been the one who has brought it to her. The servant of a wealthy woman in Chorazin arrives one day with a skein of thread for Leah. It is this woman who has bought all of Leah's thread.

21. Leah is able to show him how to make the bread.

22. Simon had had a vegetable garden behind the house, and some vegetables begin to grow among the weeds. Leah is able to help him identify the plants and separate the vegetables from the weeds.

23. Leah's recovery is very erratic, and he can't count on her health. She tires easily and is fretful, as well as being frightened by the men who come to the shop needing Daniel's services.

24. a Roman legionary

25. The Roman soldier notices Leah through the open door, and Daniel becomes angry that he will even look at his sister. It causes him to think again of the mountain and long to be there.

CHAPTERS 12-14

One afternoon a village boy enters Daniel's shop on an errand, and it is obvious the boy has been severely beaten. Although Daniel rarely interacts with those who come into his shop, he feels prompted to speak to this young man, learning he was attacked by five of his own friends because his father has gone to work for the local tax collector. Although Daniel does not approve of those who collect taxes for the Romans, he understands the boy's dilemma. His father feels forced into his position due to failed crops and unpaid taxes. Nathan, the young man, explains his father's only other option would be to sell his sister, and his father is too softhearted to do this. Although Nathan's hatred for the Romans is obvious, he defends his father, who has been accused of pocketing tax money for himself. When he is finished, Daniel walks with Nathan, assisting him when his assailants ambush him a second time. With Daniel's help, Nathan sends the others running and Nathan becomes his first recruit for the army he intends to build and present to Rosh. Not long after this encounter, Joel enters the shop with a friend in tow. Kemuel is a young man from Capernaum who is obviously wealthy, and Daniel is initially suspicious of him. However, after getting to know him and seeing his burning desire to fight the Romans, he welcomes Kemuel. They agree to meet together the third day of each week in the smithy shop. They begin to recruit others, using the verse, "He trains my hands for war, so that my arms can bend a bow of bronze" as their password. Soon there are twenty-one of the young men. Joel wants to present them to Rosh, but Daniel is not ready. He wants to wait until he has a real army, trained and ready for war. Daniel becomes uneasy after the third meeting when the Roman legionary again appears at his shop, and seems to be appearing at times that coincide strangely with the meetings of the boys. The decision is made to move their meeting place, and one of the boys offers an abandoned watchtower on his father's farm. The change is

made, and the Roman does not appear again. Daniel feels luck is with them, but still has some gnawing uneasiness.

Daniel's main concern about the new meeting place had been the amount of time it would take him away from Leah, but he finds she adjusts to his being away much more smoothly than he had anticipated. She is beginning to gain confidence, and her health is improving. She does not tire as easily, and there is color in her cheeks. When he sells her cloth, he puts the coin in her hand, which fascinates her. He shows her how to sew it into her head scarf like the other village girls, and she wears this proudly as she works. One afternoon Daniel looks up to see Joel standing in the doorway with Thacia. She tells him she wanted to see a blacksmith's shop, and shows an interest in his shop. Daniel tells Joel of a weaver's apprentice he wants him to speak to. The young man wants to join them, but has some reservations on theological grounds. Daniel feels Joel will be better able to persuade him. Malthace offers to stay in the shop while they go, and the two young men leave. As they are returning, Joel mentions to Daniel he has been to hear Jesus again several times, and Jesus has been able to instruct him on points of the Law. Daniel is incredulous, and asks how that can be since Jesus is merely a carpenter and Joel is a scholar. Joel replies he does not know where Jesus learned what He knows, but He is able to explain things like no one Jesus has ever heard. As the two young men approach the blacksmith shop, Daniel hears voices, then Thacia's laughter. He cannot believe what he is hearing. Going through the house, he finds the two young women in the garden, sitting together on a bench. Leah is delighted, exclaiming to Daniel that Thacia has come to see her. Thacia remarks on what a lovely visit they have had, and how Leah has shown her the vegetable garden. Daniel doesn't understand how this can happen – Leah has not allowed anyone to look at her for almost ten years. When he blurts out,

"What could you talk about?" Thacia responds, "You." When Joel comes through the inner door, the spell is broken. Leah is visibly frightened, and Thacia motions him away. She takes her girdle and hands it to Leah, asking her to promise not to forget her. After their visit, Daniel realizes he has paid no attention to Leah's clothing. Even though she is weaving luxurious cloth, Leah is wearing old rags. The next day, he goes to the marketplace, ill prepared to bargain for cloth. Buying blue cloth that he has been charged too much for, Daniel takes his prize to Leah. For two days she treasures the cloth itself. Finally he takes the needle and makes an attempt at threading it. Leah laughs out loud at his clumsy attempt, taking it from him and asking if he would be angry if she made herself a new dress with the cloth.

As Daniel and Leah sit over their breakfast, Leah asks what a wedding is. The night before, Daniel had attended Nathan's wedding, and now he tries to explain to his sister what that means. He wonders if their grandmother had ever talked to Leah. She knows nothing of life outside the walls of the house. At first, Daniel had spoken very little to Leah. Eventually he began speaking to her in the same way he had spoken to Samson; basically speaking his thoughts out loud. At first she listens in silence, then begins to ask questions about all he says. After Thacia's visit, the questions become more frequent, as well as more disquieting for Daniel. Daniel realizes that Leah sees the world through what he tells her, so he tries to be patient and describe all that has transpired at the wedding. When he describes the food, he chides himself for not bringing some to her. When he describes the merrymaking of all the guests, even the description is frightening to Leah. She asks if Nathan's bride will live with him, and Daniel replies she will, just as their father and mother lived together. She wants to know what will happen to her when Daniel marries, and he responds that is foolishness. He lives only to rid their land of the Roman masters. He realizes his voice is loud and angry. Leah asks if the Romans are their masters, and Daniel asks if she does not even know that. She asks if the soldier who comes to the shop is a Roman, and Daniel

replies he is. She asks if he is Daniel's master, and Daniel tells her to ask him – he would say he was. She tells Daniel that is silly. He is just a boy, and is homesick besides. Daniel becomes furious, then wonders where Leah learned such a word. Throughout the day, Daniel's anger continues to rise. When evening comes, he banks the fire and tells Leah to bar the door; he will be away. She asks if he will come back, and he assure her he will. He goes to the mountain and freedom. When he reaches the camp, he finds his reception somewhat less than his expectations. He is barely noticed. He realizes something is missing, and cannot find Samson. The large man shows up with a huge sheep, and the men have a feast. Rosh asks him about Joel, telling him to keep an eye on him. Daniel feels guilt over the sheep, knowing now the men who own all the flocks. As he tries to sleep, images of Leah alone, Joel reading from the scripture, Thacia standing in the doorway, and Simon offering him all he had come into his mind. Early in the morning, Daniel starts back to the village. Samson tries to follow, but he gestures to him to remain behind. He feels he cannot take the large black man into the village. When he returns home, he finds Leah disheveled and lifeless. He takes the water jar and feels trapped once again.

SUGGESTED ACTIVITIES CHAPTERS 12-14

1. In Chapter 12, Daniel responds to the injustice Nathan experiences by coming to his aid and physically fighting against the bullies who have beaten the young man. Assign an essay in which students either describe specific injustices they have experienced and how they were resolved, or give alternative suggestions for handling the situation faced by Nathan and Daniel.

2. Daniel attends Nathan's wedding in Chapter 14. Ask students to research Jewish wedding customs. If it is possible, visit a synagogue or have a rabbi speak to the class. If not, (delphiresearchgroup.com/weddings/resources/customs) is one site which describes both modern customs as well as those that have survived for centuries.

3. Divide students into groups. Have each group choose a verse from the Bible to describe how they want their group to be identified, and develop an illustration (like the bronze bow) that can be used as a password and a visual key to their group.

4. Have students illustrate Leah and Thacia together in the garden.

VOCABULARY CHAPTERS 12-14

scythe	(n)	an implement consisting of a long, curved single-edged blade with a long bent handle, used for mowing or reaping
waning	(v)	to grow gradually smaller or less
surly	(adj)	a rude unfriendly disposition
savoring	(v)	taste appreciatively
disdain	(n)	lack of respect accompanied by a feeling of intense dislike
whetting	(v)	make keen or more acute
warily	(adv)	careful in guarding against danger or deception
recompense	(n)	payment or reward (as for service rendered)
enchanted	(adj)	influenced as by charms or incantations
intricacy	(adj)	having elaborately complex detail
scandalous	(adj)	shocking
disconcerted	(adj)	thrown into confusion
flout	(v)	to treat with contemptuous disregard

QUESTIONS CHAPTERS 12-14

1. How does Daniel meet Nathan? Why is Daniel drawn to the boy?

2. Why have Nathan's friends turned against him?

3. What does Daniel do to help Nathan? What does this say about Daniel's character?

4. Who comes to visit Daniel? Who does he bring with him?

5. What is Daniel's plan for telling Rosh about his recruits?

6. As Daniel and his group of recruits continue to meet, what other event seems to coincide with their meetings? What do they do to solve this problem?

7. How does Leah respond to Daniel's absences from home?

8. Who comes with Joel when he comes to the shop?

9. What does Joel tell Daniel that surprises him?

10. While Daniel and Joel are gone, what happens that shocks Daniel?

11. By Daniel's reaction to Thacia's confession of the afternoon's topic of conversation, how is Daniel beginning to feel about Thacia?

12. What effect does Joel's presence have on Leah?

13. After Thacia's visit, what does Daniel realize he has neglected about his sister? What does he do to resolve this?

14. After Nathan's wedding, as he describes everything for Leah, what does Daniel realize about his relationship between Leah and the outside world?

15. What does Leah say to him that he finds strange?

16. When Daniel returns to the mountain, in what way is his arrival at the cave what he had imagined it would be?

17. In what way is it disappointing?

18. In what ways has Daniel changed since he was last with Rosh's band?

19. As Daniel tries to sleep, who comes to his mind as a contrast to Rosh?

20. What does Daniel discover about Leah when he returns home? How does this make him feel?

ANSWERS TO QUESTIONS CHAPTERS 12-14

1. Nathan comes into the blacksmith shop with a scythe that needs fixing, and he has obviously been beaten. Daniel likes the boy's spirit. He realizes the young man is a fighter with a strong will to succeed, even against impossible odds.

2. Nathan's father has become the new tax collector in the village; working for the Romans. This is the most despicable job there is for a Jew to hold. The rumors are already circulating that his father is "on the take" – pocketing a percentage of the money for himself.

3. Daniel walks with Nathan as he leaves, helping him take on and defeat the bullies who had beaten him earlier. Daniel, whose hatred for the Romans was so great, could have refused to help Nathan. However, he was opposed to injustice and wanted to right it, even against one whose father was helping the hated Romans.

4. Joel shows up at his shop, bringing a friend from Capernaum named Kemuel who wants to join with them in their fight against the Romans.

5. Daniel does not want to tell Rosh about the young men who are joining him until he can present a well-trained army to Rosh.

6. The young Roman soldier seems to appear at approximately the same time as their meetings; sometimes before or after the meetings, but always too near for comfort. One of their members offers an abandoned watchtower on his family's farm as a new meeting place.

7. She seems to take it in stride, and even gains new confidence as time passes.

8. Thacia

9. Joel has been to visit Jesus several time, and Jesus has explained points of the Law that Joel has not been able to understand on his own.

10. Leah allows Thacia to come in and visit with her, and when the boys return, they find the two young women sitting in the garden visiting with each other.

11. When Thacia confesses she and Leah have been talking about Daniel, he blushes, which indicates he is embarrassed by the confession. It is apparent he has romantic feelings for Thacia.

12. When Joel enters, Leah returns to her former frightened self. She is shaking and terrified, and unable to speak.

13. He realizes his sister is dressed in rags, in spite of the fact that she spends her days producing luxurious cloth for a wealthy woman. He is embarrassed when he becomes aware of how he has neglected her in this aspect. The next day, he goes to the marketplace, which is a woman's domain, pays too much for some blue cloth, and brings home cloth for her to make a dress for herself.

14. Daniel realizes that he acts as Leah's only window to the outside world. She sees everything through his descriptions of what goes on.

15. She mentions the Roman soldier is homesick, and he becomes furious while at the same time wondering how Leah has learned that word.

16. When he first arrives, there is a brief period of excitement at his arrival, some shouting and celebrating.

17. The celebration dies down quickly, and he is soon ignored. Rosh is in an ill humor, and most of the men have little to say to Daniel. Rather than feeling the welcome he is expecting, he feels he no longer belongs here in the way he did before. The one person he wants to see, Samson, is not present at first. His first real joy occurs when Samson returns to camp.

18. When they talk about taking the sheep from the flocks below, Daniel now feels guilt because he knows the owners of those flocks personally, and he can no longer feel it is Rosh's just due to take what he wants from the flocks. As he tries to sleep, he thinks of Leah bolted alone in the house. He now has feelings of responsibility. He has developed ties to Joel, Thacia and Simon. He has begun to understand what true friendship is. He has begun to compare Rosh to Jesus, and the difference in their methods and manners are beginning to make him think.

19. Jesus

20. Leah has returned to her former state; disheveled and unkempt with her eyes dull and unseeing. He feels once again that he is trapped.

CHAPTERS 15-16

Daniel finds the summer a time of happiness as he spends time going to Capernaum to take in the teachings of Jesus. Going first in answer to a request of Joel's, Daniel finds himself returning eagerly out of his own hunger. He rises before dawn and walks the three miles to the city, then returns to open his shop a little later. Simon encourages his coming, and he is able to see Joel and Thacia more often. At home, he shares the stories he has heard with Leah. She is especially drawn to the story of Jairus' daughter, who was raised from the dead. Daniel was present and saw this miracle take place. She asks to hear the story over and over. Daniel searches for the right words to describe the scenes to Leah in a way she can try to capture it all in her imagination, but it is impossible for a girl whose whole world is the inside of her house. She asks if Jesus will ever come to their village, and Daniel tells her He did once. She asks about the crowds that follow Him, if they jostle and push. Daniel asks Leah if she will go to see Jesus if He comes to their village. She does not answer him, but he is aware of changes in her. Thacia is coming to see her regularly, and it is drawing her out. Daniel notices that Leah seems to be listening for something, even as he talks to her, but he does not know what it is. Twice he has seen her run to the door and look out in the garden when rain has passed, making it sound like footsteps outside the garden wall. One afternoon when his work is slack, Daniel picks up a tiny piece of bronze from a molten mass, and shapes it into a tiny bronze bow with an arrow, making it into a brooch. He puts it away, half ashamed of it. As Daniel thinks of Jesus, he wonders if He will move against the Romans. He decides to go that night to the garden in Bethsaida.

Rosh has summoned Daniel, sending him with a message for Joel. As Daniel meets with Joel and Thacia in the space between the walls, Joel excitedly declares he will do anything Rosh demands of him. Daniel explains Herod Antipas, the tetrarch of Galilee, will be entertaining a special legation from Rome which will come to Capernaum for a banquet at the home of Mattathias the banker. Rosh wants the guest list. As Joel mulls over how to obtain the

information, he and Thacia come up with a plan in which Joel will disguise himself as a fish seller in order to gain the information from the kitchen slaves. Thacia will disguise herself as Joel and leave the city with Daniel so that, if anyone questions where Joel is, the guards at the gates will recall seeing him leave with Daniel. Thacia will be able to spend the day visiting with Leah. When they meet the next morning near the fishing boats, Daniel is amazed when he sees Thacia dressed up as Joel. Thacia is in a hurry to go, and Joel asks if they don't want to wait and hear Jesus. She replies she does not want to see him this morning. Daniel thinks it is because of the Law, which forbids a woman to wear a man's clothing, but Thacia responds that she does not want to look in His face with a lie. As they go, they talk about what Jesus means by the kingdom of God, and Thacia brings up the fact that Jesus has said they should love their enemies. Daniel becomes angry, stating that a girl could not understand such a thing. Deciding to change the subject, she asks if what Joel is doing is dangerous. Although he has misgivings, Daniel assures her Joel will be all right. As they leave the city, they meet two Roman soldiers, who force them to carry their packs. Daniel is about to refuse, but Thacia picks up one of them and carries it. Thacia has a wonderful visit with Leah, and the three enjoy a beautiful lunch together. Their afternoon is spoiled, though, when the young Roman soldier appears at the shop. Before returning Thacia to Capernaum, Daniel gives her the brooch he has made. She tells him he should be a silversmith instead of a blacksmith. He responds that he would like to try, then thanks Thacia for what she has meant to Leah. Thacia tells him she and Joel are aware of all he has done for his sister. They discuss the diagnosis of demon possession that has been made of Leah. Daniel tells Thacia that one doctor said that Leah does not want to be made well. Thacia asks if he has thought of taking Leah to Jesus, and he tells her he has, but does not see how he could get her to Capernaum without frightening her to death. Thacia tells him that if Jesus comes to the village, he must ask Him to come to Leah. Daniel asks if it is really worth bringing Leah back into this world. Thacia points out hundreds of cranes in flight, and remarks that it is "beautiful just to be alive in Galilee!" Daniel looks at her, and they suddenly realize they are holding hands. She takes her hand away, and they hurry down the road.

SUGGESTED ACTIVITIES CHAPTERS 15-16

1. Leah experiences the miracles and parables of Jesus vicariously through Daniel. Assign groups of students and have each group choose either a parable taught by Jesus, or a miracle experience by those who came to Jesus, and act it out as if they are acting it out for Leah. These groups can be the same as assigned in the previous section.

2. The Romans think nothing of requiring those they have conquered to carry their burdens, treating them as little more than beasts of burden. How does this add to the anger felt by those who are conquered? Lead a discussion paralleling this period with America's period of slavery. Are there similarities? How should people be treated?

3. Ask students to illustrate the scene described in the last pages of chapter 16.

4. Daniel gives the bronze bow he has made to Thacia in gratitude for what she has done for Leah. If you have access to materials that will allow students to make a small brooch for someone who has done something for them, have them make one and write a note expressing their gratitude for the other person's kindness.

VOCABULARY CHAPTERS 15-16

venture	(v)	proceed somewhere despite the risk of possible dangers
glimpsed	(v)	to look briefly; glance
eluded	(v)	escape, either physically or mentally
earnestness	(adj)	seriously intent and sober
extravagant	(adj)	unduly lavish; wasteful
legation	(n)	a diplomatic mission headed by a minister
toady	(v)	try to gain favor by cringing or flattering
intrigue	(n)	a secret scheme
scruples	(n)	an uneasy feeling arising from conscience or principle that tends to hinder action
lustrous	(adj)	gleaming with or as if with brilliant light; radiant
scrutiny	(n)	a careful looking over
relishing	(v)	to take pleasure in; enjoy
niggardly	(adj)	stingy in giving or spending
consignment	(n)	the delivery of goods for sale or disposal
irksome	(adj)	Causing annoyance, weariness, or vexation; tedious
reasserted	(v)	strengthen or make more firm
phalanx	(n)	a group or body (as of troops) in compact formation

QUESTIONS CHAPTERS 15-16

1.   What causes the month of Ab to be the happiest for Daniel?

2.   What does the time with Jesus do for Daniel's relationship with Leah?

3.   What does Daniel say about the story of the Good Samaritan? Look up some information about the Samaritans. Why does Daniel react the way he does to this story?

4.   What story does Leah like to hear the most? Why do you think she likes this story the most?

5.   When Daniel and Leah talk of the possibility of Jesus coming to their village, what does Daniel ask of Leah? How does she respond?

6.   Why does Daniel believe Leah has been changing?

7.   What does Daniel notice about Leah?

8.   What does Daniel make as a reminder of his purpose?

9.   What does Rosh want Joel to do?

10. What plan do Joel and Thacia conceive in order to carry out Rosh's orders?

11. Why does Thacia not want to see Jesus on this particular morning?

12. Read John 14:6. Does what this verse says support the thought that Thacia has about the way Jesus would feel about lying? Explain.

13. When Thacia asks if what Joel is doing is dangerous, and Daniel tells her he does not think it is, does he really believe what he is telling her?

14. How would you feel if you were Daniel or Thacia having to carry the Roman soldier's pack for them?

15. How does Leah respond to Thacia's explanation for her strange clothing?

16. What simile is used by Thacia to describe the way Leah is changing?

17. What does Thacia suggest Daniel do to help Leah?

18. What is Daniel's response?

19. How does Thacia respond to this?

20. Why does Daniel feel "almost grateful" to the Roman soldiers as they hurry on their way back to Capernaum?

ANSWERS TO QUESTIONS CHAPTERS 15-16

1. He goes to hear Jesus in Capernaum every day, in the morning when he can see Joel and Thacia, and sometimes in the evening when he can only hear Jesus speak and then go back to his home in the dark.

2. Because he is able to bring home to Leah all the things he has heard Jesus talking about, it gives him more to talk about with Leah, and enriches their time together. He wants her to be able to experience what he is experiencing, and tries his best to describe everything so that she will be able to grasp it all.

3. Daniel says that, "If Jesus means that Jews and Samaritans should treat each other like neighbors, that is foolish. It could never happen." The Samaritans are the remnant of the Jewish people who were left in the land when the Jews were taken into captivity in Babylon. They married the Gentiles who were brought into the land to live, making them half Jew and half Gentile. They also followed the pagan religions of those Gentiles, rather than remaining true to the God of the Israelites. Therefore, when the Jews returned from Babylon, they held the Samaritans in contempt, and there was a great deal of hatred between the two people. This is why Daniel made the statement he did.

4. Leah loves to hear the story of Jairus' daughter who was raised from the dead. She probably loves hearing this story the most because Daniel has seen this miracle first hand, and is able to testify to the fact that the girl has been fully healed. This would give her hope that there might be healing for her fears and the psychological condition that has held her captive for so long.

5. He asks her if she would go to see Jesus with him. She does not respond, but just hides behind her veil.

6. He believes she is changing as a result of Thacia's visits. He believes it is Thacia's natural ability to draw her out that is helping Leah to become more open and less fearful.

7. She is more careful about her appearance, and seems to be listening for something in particular. She sometimes has a dreamy expression on her face that seems wistful and searching.

8. He makes a tiny brooch of bronze in the shape of a bow and arrow.

9. He wants him to find out the names of men who will be attending a banquet for the tetrarch at the home of Mattathias the banker.

10. Joel will disguise himself as a fish seller in order to get information from the kitchen slaves, and Thacia will disguise herself as Joel, leaving Capernaum with Daniel in case anyone recognizes Joel. That way the guards at the gates can testify they saw Joel leaving the city.

11. She does not want Him to see her participating in a lie.

12. Jesus has declared He is the Truth. Since this is the case, He would not approve of lying in any form, so Thacia is correct in her assumption.

13. He does not believe what he is saying, but is merely trying to ease Thacia's doubts and not face his own.

14. Answers will vary.

15. She tells Thacia that Daniel never plays games.

16. Thacia says it is "like watching a flower opening very slowly."

17. She suggests that, if Jesus comes to Ketzah, Daniel should ask Him to come to his house and heal Leah.

18. He doesn't know if it is really worth bringing Leah back into a world with all the problems existing in their world.

19. She points to hundreds of cranes which are flying overhead, making a beautiful picture, and says , "It's beautiful just to be alive in Galilee."

20. As they pass the Roman soldiers, they take no notice of Daniel and Thacia. Daniel is grateful because he cannot bear the thought of Thacia having to carry a pack again like she did in the morning.

CHAPTERS 17-19

As Daniel is working at his bellows, the villagers voice their anger to him that Rosh has overstepped his bounds this time. Daniel asks how they know it was Rosh, and they reply that there is no other man in Galilee who would dare to rob five of the wealthiest homes in the city. They are amazed how he could have found out Mattathias was giving a banquet, or even that the tetrarch was even going to be in the city. Daniel asks again how they can know it is Rosh, and they tell him some of Rosh's band decided to rob the home of the centurion, and were caught. One was killed before they could question him, but the other talked before they killed him. Daniel feels ill, wondering which of the men he has lived next to for five years was killed. He defends Rosh, telling the men if Rosh robs, it is for a good reason. The men scoff at this; saying they have heard that Rosh steals from the rich to give to the poor, but the poor will never see any of what was taken from this raid. Daniel realizes more of the villagers are turning against Rosh. Daniel wonders what Joel thinks about the raid, and if he feels his part in it has been worthwhile. He does not have long to wait. When Joel attends a meeting of the village "Bronze Bow" club, he is hailed as a hero, and he is thrilled at the results of his work; making plans to continue delivering fish on a regular basis in order to glean what information he can from the centurion's slaves. Soon there is an efficient communication system set up between Joel in Capernaum and Rosh on the mountain. The information Joel gathers is smuggled out to the young men at the watchtower, then to Joktan who runs with it to the mountain and Rosh. Soon there was no one wealthy who can travel the roads of Galilee safely without fear of attack by Rosh and his men. Daniel's young men also begin to become more bold, harassing the Romans and stealing equipment from under their noses. Daniel is disgusted with what is happening, feeling the antics of the young men is childish rather than being the kind of armed activity he had been dreaming of. At one point the Romans bring a catapult down the road, guarded by only two men. Daniel's band talk him into stealing the catapult from under the noses of the Romans. Realizing they are going to

use it on Rosh, Daniel is outnumbered and allows himself to be talked into it. He warns the others not to kill the guards – he does not want to bring reprisal on the whole village. They disable the guards and dismantle the catapult throughout the night, carrying it to the watchtower piece by piece. By the morning, not a piece remains, and no one is able to find out what has become of it. The villagers come to Daniel, telling him to carry a message to Rosh to leave their sheep alone. When Daniel takes the message, he laughs in Daniel's face. He warns Rosh they will turn to the Romans for protection. Rosh tells him to let them come. Daniel despairs, knowing the village is turning against Rosh now.

On the last day of the month of Ebul (September) Thacia comes rushing into Daniel's shop grief stricken, and tells Daniel that Joel has been taken. He is being held in the garrison, and will be sent east in the morning. Distraught, she asks Daniel if that means Joel will be sentenced to the galleys; she does not believe he would survive the galleys. He touches her shoulder, reassuring her that Rosh will have a plan for this, and Thacia collapses in tears. He calls to Leah to take care of Thacia, then heads for the mountain. When he informs Rosh of Joel's plight, the man simply replies that Joel has become too overconfident. As Daniel asks about Rosh's plans for a rescue, Rosh tells him every man on the mountain is responsible for himself. Daniel reminds him that eight of them took Samson, but Rosh counters with the fact that that was from traders, not Roman soldiers. Daniel reminds Rosh that Joel has been important to them. Rosh replies that he was stupid enough to get caught, so he can't risk even one man to help to free him. Rosh brings up again that Daniel has a soft spot, and will be no good to the cause until he gets rid of it. As Daniel looks at Rosh, he sees him as he really is for the first time, and replies that Rosh does not even know what the cause is. Daniel tells him he is not one of his men, not any longer. As he turns to go, Joktan follows, asking Daniel what he will do. Daniel replies he will go after Joel, and Joktan asks if he will go by himself. Daniel replies that there are nineteen of them, and

Joktan says, no, twenty. Daniel is disappointed it was not Samson following him, but he still feels there is someone else following along. When he faces the other boys, they are discouraged that Rosh will not help, but elect Daniel their leader. Daniel lays out his plan for rescuing Joel, and they set out to take their places before dawn.

Daniel has chosen the steep banks along the Via Maris near Magdala, where the Romans will not be expecting an attack. Daniel's instructions are for the boys to wait for the mounted soldiers to pass, then they are to assail the guards with rocks and what weapons they have. Daniel will jump down and free Joel from his shackles. Nathan is to help them up, and they will all be off, trying to engage the Romans as little as possible. Daniel does not expect to survive, but he intends to make sure Joel is saved. By midafternoon, Joktan spots the entourage on its way, and gives warning. Daniel waits until Joel is nearly below them, then gives the signal. Daniel realizes with dismay the Romans are charging up the sides of the banks, and they are not going to be able to hold them off. Suddenly a huge boulder comes from the other side, and Daniel is confused – there was no one stationed on the other side. As he watches, Samson comes swinging down into the fracas. Daniel jumps, taking out the guard near Joel and starting to work on his shackles. That is the last thing he remembers. He is jerked upward and thrown like a sack. He loses consciousness. When he awakens, Joel is sitting near him and Kemuel warns him not to move. He thinks Daniel has a broken shoulder bone and some broken ribs. Daniel feels an odd shape on his head, and Joel tells him his irons hit him there. Daniel is confused, thinking the Romans jumped him. Joel and Kemuel tell him it was Samson who grabbed him and tore open Joel's irons, then threw the two boys up on the ledge. Daniel asks where Samson is. Joel tells him he was wounded. He was hit by a spear before they left. Kemuel assures Daniel he won't have to worry about the galleys. Samson will not live to reach the coast. Daniel turns his head away, and sees Nathan's body. Kemuel explains Nathan leaned too far out when trying to pull him down. Daniel is sick, thinking of Nathan's new bride waiting for him at home. He asks how many more. Kemuel asks if he can walk, and they make it to the meeting place. All are accounted for except for Nathan. They now have a new respect for the might of Rome. They know that without Samson they would not have been able to have freed Joel.

SUGGESTED ACTIVITIES CHAPTERS 17-19

THERE ARE NO SUGGESTED ACTIVITIES FOR THESE SECTIONS.

VOCABULARY CHAPTERS 17-19

defrauded	(v)	deprive of by deceit
indignant	(adj)	angered at something unjust or wrong
garnered	(v)	assemble or get together
swarthy	(adj)	dark in color or complexion
bereft	(adj)	deprived of or lacking something
routed	(v)	to defeat decisively
flaunted	(v)	to show off
patronized	(v)	to act as a patron to; support or sponsor
reprisal	(n)	an act in retaliation for something done by another
fissure	(n)	a narrow opening or crack
oblique	(adj)	having a slanting or sloping direction, course, or position; inclined
foreboding	(n)	a feeling of evil to come

QUESTIONS CHAPTERS 17-19

1. What has Rosh done with the information gathered by Joel?

2. Read Exodus 20:15; Ephesians 4:28; Titus 2:10 and 1 Peter 4:15. What does the Bible say about stealing? In that light, could Rosh be the Messiah? Why or why not?

3. What has happened to the way the people of the village feel about Rosh?

4. How does Daniel feel about what has happened by the end of the day? Does he feel that what Rosh has done has anything to do with raising an army to overthrow the Romans?

5. How does Joel feel about what he has done? What decision does he make?

6. How are messages relayed from Joel to Rosh? What happens after Rosh receives a message?

7. What seems apparent about Rosh to everyone except for the boys who are so loyal to him?

8. When the boys steal the Roman catapult, how does Daniel show that Simon's words to him have made an impression?

9. What message is given to Daniel to take to Rosh? How does Rosh respond to this message?

10. When Thacia comes to tell Daniel Joel has been taken, what thought comes to Daniel's mind?

11. When Daniels goes to Rosh for help, how does Rosh respond?

12. What does Daniel realize about Rosh?

13. What is Daniel's plan for rescuing Joel?

14. When the boys elect him as their leader, how does Daniel feel?

15. Why does the attack not go as Daniel had planned?

16. Who comes down from the other side?

17. When Daniel awakens, what does he learn about how he and Joel were able to get up the bank from the road?

18. What has happened to Nathan?

19.   What happened to Samson?

20.   How have the boys changed in their respect for the Roman soldiers?

ANSWERS TO QUESTIONS CHAPTERS 17-19

1. Rosh and his men have looted the homes of the people who were guests at the banquet   at the home of Mattathias' house.

2. Scripture forbids stealing; listing it as one of the commandments in the Ten Commandments. In the New Testament, Paul instructs the Ephesians that those who have stolen in the past should not steal any more now that they are Christians. Because stealing is a sin, the Messiah would not be participating in it. Rosh shows himself as one who loves himself and is out to indulge himself, and this does not fulfill the requirements for the Messiah. He is required to be without sin (Jeremiah 23:5), and Rosh would definitely not fulfill that requirement.

3. The people in the village feel Rosh has gone too far.

4. Daniel feels dull and let down. He had thought the mission Joel had been sent on would amount to something more noble than just looting the homes of the wealthy Jews in the community. No, Daniel doesn't feel this has anything to do with the cause.

5. Joel is excited about what he has done, and is so carried away by his success at disguising himself he decides to continue going to the centurion's home twice a week disguised as a fisherman.

6. Joel manages to get the message to one of the band, who relays it to the watchtower. Joktan brings it from the watchtower to the mountain.

7. Rosh is nothing but a common thief, caring only for himself and what he can take from   those who have wealth.

8. He admonishes the boys not to kill the guards, or they will bring the wrath of Rome down on the entire village.

9. Two of the villagers tell Daniel to carry a message to Rosh to stop stealing their sheep. Rosh laughs at Daniel when he gives him the message; telling Daniel the men are afraid of their own shadows and they are not good for anything other than raising food for Rosh and his men.

10. When Thacis says she Knew from the beginning Joel would be taken, Daniel thinks to himself that he knew it also.

11. Rosh tells him that Joel was overconfident; he was caught because he was stupid, and he is responsible for his own actions.

12. He realizes Rosh is not the hero he has thought he was, and recognizes him for what he truly is.

13. Daniel has chosen the steep banks along the Via Maris near Magdala, where the Romans will not be expecting an attack. Daniel's instructions are for the boys to wait for the mounted soldiers to pass, then they are to assail the guards with rocks and what weapons they have. Daniel will jump down and free Joel from his shackles. Nathan is to help them up, and they will all be off, trying to engage the Romans as little as possible.

14. He feels "only a cold heaviness." The weight of the responsibility of leadership is greater than he had anticipated.

15. The Roman soldiers are more well trained than Daniel had anticipated, and they are   not so easily routed. He had expected the Romans to retreat quickly when they were   assailed with the rocks, and instead they used their shields, closed ranks and began   to assail the banks.

16. Samson

17. He learns that Samson came down, opened Joel's chains, and threw both Daniel an Joel up on the ledge.

18. Nathan is killed in the battle.

19. Samson was injured in the attack by the Romans, and was taken by them when they left. Kemuel assures Daniel it was a fatal wound.

20. They now have a much higher regard for the strength of the Roman army and their ability to cause damage that is well beyond what Daniel and his league of young men can hope to counter. They are aware that they would never have been able to even free Joel without the help of Samson.

CHAPTERS 20-22

During the month of Tishri (October) the boys have disbanded, being careful not to be seen together too often in public. Daniel works to the limits of his ability in the blacksmith's shop, but his broken bones do not allow him to work off his anger the way he desires. The boys declare they will begin meeting again soon, but they have lost the conviction in their words; their faith in Rosh is gone. Daniel had heard Jesus say, "They who live by the sword will perish by the sword." At the time, Daniel accepted that as an honorable death. He could think of no better way to die than as a warrior defending the freedom of his nation. However, the battle had not gone as he had supposed. Samson and Nathan had died, and he felt the responsibility for their deaths. To make things even worse, his actions had done nothing to bring freedom even an iota closer. The one gain from Daniel's exploit is Joktan. He has inserted himself into life in the village as if he had always been there, and has begun to work as Daniel's apprentice. Nine days have passed, and Daniel has heard nothing from Joel. He is beginning to wonder what has happened to his friend, and whether Joel regrets the vow he has taken. Late one evening, there is a knock at the door, and a stranger stands in the rain outside. When Daniel answers the door, the man pushes his way inside, and it turns out to be Joel. Joel tells him his father has not let him out for fear he will be recognized and arrested again. Daniel thinks Joel's father must hate him, but Joel tells him his father tells him he can come to the house whenever he wants. He is grateful to Daniel for saving Joel. Joel tells Daniel he has left without telling his father, intending to go to the mountain to live with Rosh. Daniel asks why, and Joel responds that his father is sending him to Jerusalem to school. Since this is what Joel has always wanted, Daniel asks why he would give it all up. He tells Daniel he wants to work for the victory. Daniel informs Joel he has broken with Rosh. Joel tells him he should not do that because of him, but Daniel replies it would have happened anyway. Rosh was doing

things to weaken the Jewish people, not the Romans. Joel tells him a new leader will come, and they must be ready. Daniel tells him yes, but they will need the priests and scribes, too, as well as the farmers and laborers. Joel tells him he would like to do it for his father, also; he wants his father to be proud of him. Joel tells Daniel he has brought a gift from Thacia to Leah. He asks if he can give the gift to Leah himself. Daniel responds that, since Leah has seen him from the door, she might take it from him. Joel hands the gift to Leah, even though she is trembling. When he returns from the room, Daniel remarks Joel is the only person other than Thacia who has come near Leah. Joel tells Daniel he also has a message from Thacia for him. In four days, on the Day of Atonement, Thacia will dance and sing in the vineyard with the other girls. She wants Daniel to come. He responds he would not know how to act. Joel goes on to describe Thacia's current condition to Daniel, telling him she is having difficulty dealing with being confined in the house. Joel feels his parents have given her too much freedom. Their father is putting pressure on Thacia to choose a husband – she is sixteen and should already be married. Daniel knows what Joel is implying, but tells Joel Thacia must choose one of her own kind. Joel asks about him, and he replies he cannot take a wife, as he has sworn a vow of vengeance. Joel adds that Jesus needs to be warned that the elders of the synagogue want to kill Him. He begs Daniel to go to Jesus and warn Him. As Joel leaves, Daniel feels it is the end of everything, and is in despair.

Daniel delivers Joel's warning about Jesus to Simon, but Simon tells him Jesus already is aware of this information. Seeing Daniel's annoyance at his reaction, Simon tries to smooth Daniel's ruffled feathers. He explains that Jesus knows the priests are trying to trap Him, even though they have made no move toward Him. Daniel asks why Jesus stays if He knows He is in danger, and Simon replies the people need

Him. The door is shut and Daniel is left in the garden. Knowing he has used bringing the warning as an excuse to try and speak to Jesus himself, Daniel continues to stay in the garden. Andrew comes to the door, announcing Jesus is too tired to see anyone else, setting off a wailing of the sick and lame who are camped outside the door. The door opens again to allow Jesus, Andrew and Simon to leave. Jesus touches a few of those gathered in the garden, then retires to the roof of the house. Although Daniel does not believe he has made a noise, Jesus asks who is there, calling Daniel up to Him. Jesus asks why Daniel is troubled, and Daniel explains he came to warn Jesus He is in danger. Thanking him for the warning, Jesus again asks what is troubling him, and Daniel allows all of the grief of the past few weeks to spill out. Jesus asks what Daniel lives for, and Daniel replies he lives for freedom for his people and vengeance for his parents. He explains how things have gone wrong, and now he has another debt to pay – that of Samson's life. Jesus asks if Samson was his friend. Daniel realizes he has never thought of Samson that way – only as a burden, or a symbol of his weakness, but he realizes Samson has been a friend to him. Jesus explains that Samson has given all he had for Daniel, and he gave it in love. Jesus asks how Daniel can repay that kind of love with hate. Daniel cannot see how he can love the Romans, and Jesus explains that hate is the enemy. Only love is greater than hate. Daniel pleads with Jesus to lead them against the Romans, asking how long they must wait, and Jesus asks Daniel to follow Him. Daniel pledges to fight for Jesus until the end. Jesus asks if he would love for Him until the end. Jesus tells him he must give up his hate for the kingdom of God. Daniel replies he has taken a vow, and asks if a vow is not sacred. Jesus asks what his vow was. Daniel replies "To fight! To live and die for God's Victory!" Jesus smiles, telling him that is not a vow of hate. He assures him he is not far from the kingdom of God.

On the fifteenth Day of Tishri, the Day of Atonement, the shops are closed. The pious Jews are moving to the synagogue while others are celebrating in a more frivolous way. Joktan has asked for the day off, and Daniel has given him permission, so he has gone to enjoy the festivities. About noontime, Daniel asks Leah if she will go with him to see Thacia dance in the vineyard. She asks if he is going, saying he can tell her all about it. He asks again, but she tells him not to tease her. He finally mumbles he has to take a lock and key to old Omar. Leah takes his clean woolen cloak from the chest, as everyone will be in their best clothing. Although everyone is laughing, Daniel's angry scowl keeps anyone from approaching him. As Daniel nears the vineyard, he sees the ring of girls dressed in white with flowers in their hair, surrounded by boys who are obviously wealthy. Daniel realizes he does not belong. However, he is enthralled with Thacia's grace. He turns away before she can reach him, but she comes after him, asking if he still considers her a pretty child. She makes it obvious how much she cares for him, but he tells her there is no room in his life for anyone else. He has only room for his vow. Although she is hurt, she tells him "God go with you whatever you do." When he reaches the house, Leah wants him to tell her all about Thacia; what she looked like and what the dance was like. Daniel picks up some blossoms and puts them in her hair, and she begins to dance. He smiles at her, telling her she should have been dancing with them – she is as pretty as any of them. She asks if he really thinks so, and his answer seems important to her. She tells him Thacia said she was pretty, too, and asks if anyone else could think she was pretty besides him and Thacia. Daniel tells her Joel has said so, too, but that is not the answer she is looking for. She tells him his supper is ready, and she has a surprise for him. After he eats vegetables from her garden, she brings out a woven basket of fruit. The fruit is fine fruit – pomegranates, and juicy figs that are not usually found on normal Galilean tables. He asks where she got the fruit; if it was payment for her weaving. She tells him it was a gift from Marcus. He asks who Marcus is, and she replies he is the Roman soldier who has come to the shop. In his rage, he sends the fruit flying and terrorizes Leah. He demands to know how she knows his name. She tells him he has been her friend since the previous summer. He becomes angrier, asking if she let a Roman in his house. She replies he only sits on his horse outside the garden wall and talks to her. He asks what they have talked about, and she replies he has talked about his family in Gallia, who have yellow hair like hers. He forces Leah to promise never to talk to him again, and goes out to walk in the rain. As he walks, he realizes it was last summer when she said the soldier was homesick. He also realizes Rome means nothing to Leah. She had merely seen a boy close to her own age with hair like hers, and had talked to him. Daniel resolves to make it up to Leah, so she will not be afraid of him any longer. When he returns to the house, she is in the corner, but does not raise her head.

SUGGESTED ACTIVITIES CHAPTERS 20-22

1. Although Joel comes to Daniel in the story, tell students to write a letter as if Joel is not able to get away to come to Daniel, and has to write to him instead to explain how he feels and what is happening to him.

2. Have students act out the dance in the vineyard on the Day of Atonement.

3. Ask students to research the meaning of the Day of Atonement. What is its significance to the Jews, and how does it relate to Christians?

VOCABULARY CHAPTERS 20-22

scribes	(n)	a scholar of Jewish law in New Testament times
blasphemy	(n)	the act of expressing lack of reverence for God
pious	(adj)	devoutly religious
frivolous	(adj)	lacking in seriousness
dourly	(adv)	silently ill-humored; gloomy
amends	(n)	compensation for injury or loss
preoccupation	(n)	complete absorption of the mind or interests
scrabbling	(v)	scrape or grope about frenetically with the hands
cowered	(v)	to shrink or crouch down from fear or cold
averted	(v)	to turn aside or away
loathing	(v)	hate coupled with disgust
groveling	(v)	to behave in a servile or demeaning manner; cringe
intermittent	(adj)	coming and going at intervals

QUESTIONS CHAPTERS 20-22

1. What has happened to the band of boys since the incident on the road with the Romans?

2. What words of Jesus have become too real to Daniel? Why do they not mean what he thought they would mean?

3. What positive effect has Daniel gained from the experience?

4. What questions does he have about Joel?

5. When Joel comes, what does he tell Daniel about the way his father feels toward Daniel?

6. What does Joel plan to do?

7. What does Daniel tell him?

8. What is Joel's response when Daniel tells him Rosh is no longer their leader?

9. How does Leah respond when Daniel tells her Joel has brought her a gift from Thacia?

10. What does Joel tell Daniel about Thacia? What is his intention? What is Daniel's response?

11. What is the last thing Joel asks of Daniel?

12. When Daniel takes Joel's message to Jesus, what happens?

13. Why does Daniel continue to hang around the garden?

14. What does Jesus say to Daniel that is difficult for him to understand?

15. When Daniel repeats his vow for Jesus, why does He tell Daniel he is not far from the kingdom?

16. What excuse does Daniel use to go to the city on the Day of Atonement?

17. Why does he feel out of place?

18. What is Thacia desiring from Daniel? Why does he not feel he can give it?

19. How does Leah respond when Daniel tells her how pretty she is?
20. When Daniel discovers Leah's relationship with Marcus, the Roman soldier, how does he react? After his anger abates, what does he realize?

ANSWERS TO QUESTIONS CHAPTERS 20-22

1. They are no longer meeting, and are afraid to be seen together in public. They still speak of getting together again after things have cooled off, but they no longer truly believe they will truly see anything decisive in the near future. They have lost faith in Rosh, and have lost faith that things will change.

2. "They who live by the sword will die by the sword." He had thought of the glory of dying as a warrior, of dying in battle as he fought to right what was wrong. However, it is not Daniel who has died, but Samson and Nathan. Instead of feeling there is something glorious about it, he feels responsible for ending their deaths.

3. Joktan has come down from Rosh's band of outlaws and has joined Daniel, working with him in his blacksmith shop.

4. He wonders what has happened to Joel; whether Joel is in danger; what Joel thinks about what happened that night; and whether he regrets taking the vow against the Romans. He wonders if being in chains has shaken Joel's sense of purpose.

5. Joel tells Daniel his father is grateful to Daniel for saving Joel's life, and Daniel is welcome at their house anytime.

6. Joel tells Daniel he has run away from his father's house to join Rosh.

7. Daniel tells him to go to Jerusalem and study to be a great scholar, as they will need scholars when the true leader comes.

8. Joel does not want Daniel to break with Rosh for his sake, but Daniel explains how they have seen what Rosh is doing – stealing from the Jews and weakening their own people rather than weakening the Romans.

9. She is fearful and trembling, but allows Joel to come into the room and place the gift on the chest.

10. Joel tells Daniel that their father has given Thacia too much freedom, and now it is time for her to choose a husband. Their parents have promised not to make a pre-arranged marriage for them, but to allow them to choose their own spouse. Joel tells Daniel Thacia wants him to come to the vineyard to see her dance on the Day of Atonement. Joel's intention is to let Daniel know how much Thacia cares for him. He wants to feel Daniel out and see how he will respond. Daniel tells Joel Thacia should choose a husband from among her own kind – he has taken a vow of vengeance, and has no room in his life for a wife.

11. He wants Daniel to get a message to Jesus that the leaders of the synagogue are seeking a reason to have Jesus put to death.

12. Daniel is not allowed to get into where Jesus is, and Simon lets him know that Jesus is already aware of the threat against Him.

13. He feels the need to talk to Jesus, and continues to stay in hopes he will get to talk to Him.

14. Jesus tells Daniel that his real enemy is hatred, and that He asks Daniel to love for Him until the end, rather than to fight for Him until the end.

15. When Daniel tells Jesus that their vow was "to live and die for God's Victory," Jesus knows that Daniel has unwittingly vowed a vow that was not full of hatred, but full of life. Living for God's victory is what is expected of all who follow Him, and Romans 12:1-2 reveals that those who live for Him also die daily for Him, although Daniel could not actually understand this yet.

16. He needs to deliver a lock and key to a customer.

17. When he arrives at the vineyard, all of the young people who are there are obviously wealthy, and he is obviously only of the working class. He does not feel he belongs with this group that is so much better off than he.

18. Thacia wants Daniel to pledge his love to her, but he cannot do it for the same reason he gave to Joel. He feels the vengeance in his life takes precedence over everything else.

19. She wants to know if anyone other than he and Thacia would think she is pretty, and seems to be preoccupied.

20. He becomes full of rage, and takes it out on Leah, terrifying her. Once he has cooled down, he realizes that Leah has simply seen a young man who is barely older than her with blond hair like hers, and has been drawn to him because of their similarities. He does not understand why she was not afraid of the Roman, but he does know she is afraid of him now.

CHAPTERS 23-24

After Daniel's tirade, Leah has reverted to her former state, and is unable to do anything other than cower in the corner. The one thing that has changed is that she now fears Daniel. Trying to make amends, Daniel does all the work in the house, preparing food for Leah and trying to coax her to eat. She refuses to eat in his presence, and when he leaves the food for her it is often only half eaten. Daniel is convinced Leah is totally possessed by demons. At some point he latches onto the hope that Jesus will be able to help her, and goes to Capernaum to seek Him. When he arrives, he finds the fishing boats deserted, and an old man who is lame tells him they have all gone to the plain. Following the directions of those he meets, Daniel realizes a very large crowd has passed this way. As he reaches the edge of the crowd, he hears people saying, "It is the Messiah!" Daniel thinks Jesus must have declared Himself, and is filled with joy. He asks someone what Jesus has said, and the man tells him Jesus has fed them all. Finally he sees Simon, and asks where Jesus is. Simon tells him Jesus is gone. Daniel is incredulous. He does not understand why Jesus would not accept a crown. Simon tells him he does not understand, but it is not time, and Jesus wants to be alone in the mountains. Daniel asks what sort of man He is, and Simon replies He is the Messiah. Daniel asks when He will lead them against the enemy, and Simon tells Daniel He never will. Daniel asks what Jesus has offered that is worth more than Israel's freedom, and Simon replies, "He has offered me the kingdom." Daniel does not understand this statement, and asks how Simon can say he has the kingdom when nothing is changed, but Simon tells him it will be changed. God has not forgotten Israel. He has sent Jesus and Simon knows he is safe. Daniel scoffs that Jesus has put them all in danger. He asks Simon how he knows he is not risking his life for nothing. Simon replies that he believes Jesus' promises. Daniel is finished with promises, and stumbles

away in despair. He feels he has nothing left but his hatred and his vow.

As the spring comes, Daniel throws himself into his work, and Leah remains unchanged. Daniel feels he is stronger than Leah because of the hatred that drives him. He feels that if he were free from Leah, he would find a band of Zealots and join them. However, he feels chained to the forge and to this girl who does not care whether she lives or not. During the first month of spring, Leah receives her last blow. Her little goat gives birth, then becomes ill with a fever and dies. Leah becomes ill with the fever, hallucinating and crying out as she suffers. Daniel calls for the physician, who comes reluctantly, but says there is nothing he can do. Telling a customer he cannot work due to his sister's fever, Daniel bolts the door. Word travels quickly, and neighbors stay away. As he sits beside Leah's mat, he feels that all who have been a part of his life have left. When Leah dies, he will be free, but he suddenly feels terrified of a life devoid of everything except hate. The words of Jesus come to him, "Can you repay love with vengeance?" He knew Leah had loved him, just as Samson had loved him. Just like Samson, Leah would die by the same sword he meant for Rome. He suddenly thinks he should get word to Thacia, the only person who will care. Sending a message by Joktan, Daniel continues to tend to Leah for three days. Three times a day he goes to the well for water, bathing her hands and face. On the second day, he sees Marcus standing in front of his house. He resolves to kill the boy after Leah's death. Marcus places himself in front of Daniel, asking how Leah is doing. On the third day when Daniel returns from the well, Marcus approaches, telling him he must speak to him. He tells him he understands his hate, as he is German. His people have also been conquered by the Romans. Daniel tells him he should have died before he served him. Marcus tells him his cohort is being transferred, and he hopes never to see this land again. However, Leah is the only good thing that has happened to him here. He asks to see her before he goes. Daniel replies that he will not profane his house. Daniel enters the house, and Leah is so silent he thinks at first she is dead. She is barely alive, and he falls asleep. When he awakens, Jesus is entering the house followed by Thacia. Jesus sits down, motioning for Daniel and Thacia to also sit. Jesus looks at Daniel, and Daniel knows He understands everything. Jesus smiles, and Daniel desires to give up everything to follow Him. He tries to cling to the words of David, "He trains my hands for war" Daniel wonders if only love can bend the bow of bronze. Simon had told him he had to choose Jesus, even if he did not fully understand. Making the choice, Daniel feels a new peace. Thacia takes his hand, and points to Leah, who is awakening as if from a deep sleep. She asks Jesus if it is all right, and He tells her not to be afraid. For the first time since his childhood, Daniel cries. Leah tells him she knows what Jairus' daughter must have felt like. He tells her he does too. Daniel rushes out the door, trying to follow Jesus to thank him. Seeing Marcus across the street, Daniel goes to him instead and tells him Leah is better, and invites him into his house.

SUGGESTED ACTIVITIES CHAPTERS 23-24

1.   Although the Romans were the first to send troops so far away from their homes, they were not the last. If possible, invite a veteran or veterans who have served the military in wartime. Rather than asking for their war experiences, ask them to share a time when someone was kind to them, as Leah was kind to Marcus and made him feel less homesick.

2.   Of course, chapter twenty-four records Daniel's surrender of his heart and will to Jesus. Give students the opportunity to volunteer to give testimony of how they came to accept Jesus as Savior. If there are students who are not Christ believers, this might present an opportunity for them to be open to the Gospel.

3.   Ask students to write a short story projecting the characters of the story into the future, after the fall of Jerusalem and the scattering of the Jews. What has happened to Daniel, Thacia, Joel and Leah? Where are they living? Have any of them joined any of the Christian groups mentioned in the Bible? Since they are fictional characters, they can take them anywhere they want.

VOCABULARY CHAPTERS 23-24

wan	(adj)	unnaturally pale, as from physical or emotional distress
remorse	(n)	a gnawing distress arising from a sense of guilt for past wrongs
tumult	(n)	a state of commotion and noise and confusion
parched	(adj)	to make extremely dry, especially by exposure to heat
concoction	(n)	something created (a medicine or drink or soup etc.) by compounding or mixing a variety of components
rue	(n)	a European strong-scented woody herb with bitter-tasting leaves
profane	(v)	to treat (something sacred) with irreverence or contempt

QUESTIONS CHAPTERS 23-24

1. What is the result of Daniel's tirade?

2. What does Daniel try to do to make up for how he has hurt Leah? Does it help?

3. What does he decide he needs to do?

4. What does Daniel discover when he arrives in Capernaum?

5. When he finds Jesus, what is happening?

6. Why is Daniel disappointed?

7. Why does Daniel feel he is stronger than Leah?

8. What does he think he would do if he were free from having to take responsibility for Leah?

9. What happens that is the final blow to Leah?

10. As Leah lies dying, what does Daniel realize as he contemplates her life that is slipping away?

11. Whose words come to his heart?

12. When Marcus speaks to Daniel to explain his situation, what does he tell him?

13. Why does he care about Leah?

14. What is it about Marcus's request that angers Daniel the most?

15. Why do you think this causes Daniel to be angry?

16. At what point does the climax of the book occur?

17. When Leah tells Daniel she knows how Jairus' daughter felt, why does Daniel say he does too?

18. What is the new vow that Daniel and Thacia make?

19. When Daniel tells Marcus about Leah, what does he realize about the boy?

20. What do you think Daniel and Leah will tell Marcus when he comes into the house? How do you think he will receive their message?

ANSWERS TO QUESTIONS CHAPTERS 23-24

1. Leah has returned to the same condition she was in when Daniel first found her when their grandmother was dying. All of the progress she has made is gone, except now she is afraid of Daniel, as well.

2. He does all of the work in the house, and tries to be extra patient with her, coaxing her gently to eat her food and trying to get some response from her. It does not help at all.

3. He decides to go to Jesus for help.

4. The fishing boats are all deserted and all of the people are gone. As Daniel follows the directions of people along the way, he finally finds a large crowd.

5. Jesus has just fed the crowd of over five thousand and they have tried to declare Him King. However, He has slipped away from them to go away in solitude in the mountains.

6. He now feels he has no one to follow. He has no true friend, and there is nothing left for him but his vow and his hatred.

7. Although they have both lost everything, Leah has given up but Daniel is driven even harder. He feels that he has more hatred than before, and his hatred gives him a strength and purpose that Leah does not have.

8. He would find a band of Zealots and join them.

9. Her little goat, the only living thing she has left to love, becomes sick with the fever and dies.

10. He has lost everyone who has been a part of his life, and if Leah dies he will have no ties to anyone. He will be free, but total freedom with nothing but hatred to fill his life suddenly becomes terrifying.

11. The words Jesus said to him about Samson.

12. Marcus is German; his people were conquered by the Romans just like the Jews. He serves in the army because the Germans are warriors, and serving in the army gives him Roman citizenship.

13. He has been lonely and miserable while serving in Israel, and only Leah's kindness has helped him to tolerate his time here.

14. Daniel is angered by the fact that Marcus has humbled himself to even ask to see Leah.

15. Daniel realizes what it has taken for Marcus to humble himself before Daniel, and this makes him all the more angry because he knows that his pride would never allow him to do the same to Marcus.

16. The climax occurs when Daniel gives up his hatred and chooses instead to accept Jesus, follow Him and choose love rather than hatred and pride.

17. Although Leah has been physically raised from a near death condition, Daniel has been "born again." He has experienced the truth of Galatians 2:20 – his old self has died, but he has been made new through the power of Christ.

18. They have made a vow of love to each other.

19. Marcus sobs when Daniel tells him.

20. They will tell him the message of Jesus. He will probably be more receptive, having seen the change that has been affected in Daniel's attitude and actions

VOCABULARY TEST CHAPTERS 1-2
THE BRONZE BOW

I. **Fill in the blank: Fill in the blank with the correct vocabulary word, using the word bank at the end of this section:**

1. Daniel remembered that in every _____ in a stone wall, there would have burst a springtime flower.

2. When he saw the Joel and Malthace, he was like an animal _____ out of hiding, edging slowly from behind the rock.

3. All at once his attention was _____ by the Romans passing below.

4. Daniel told Rosh's men he would _____ for Joel.

5. Those in the caravan knew they were approaching a place that was lonely, narrow and _____.

6. The large slave stood like a beast of stone, _____ that he had exchanged one master for another.

7. When Daniel had taken a deliberate _____ for himself, he took the gourd of water to the slave.

8. When the man snatched the mutton from his hands, he sank his teeth into it with a _____ which turned Daniel's stomach.

9. The slave crouched in a sort of _____ after his meal.

10. Daniel told Samson that Rosh did not leave anything to chance, not the slightest _____.

Word Bank:

vouch	ferocity	cranny	trifle	draught
diverted	stupor	indifferent	lured	treacherous

II. Multiple Choice: Circle the letter of the correct answer:

1. Daniel had eyes that could light with fierce **patriotism**:
    a. pride based on family heritage
    b. state absorbed into a smaller one
    c. love of & devotion to one's country
    d. hatred for one's enemies

2. Looking down into the valley, Daniel could see the olive trees splashed with **burgeoning** thickets of oleander:
    a. falling into decay
    b. growing and flourishing
    c. refusing to budge
    d. falling back

3. Joel's young face was **taut**, and his hands were clenched:
    a. impatient
    b. relaxed
    c. pleasingly appropriate
    d. extremely nervous; tense

4. The cause of the **fracas** stood motionless in the middle of the path:
    a. failure to negotiate peace
    b. noisy, disorderly fight or quarrel; brawl
    c. partnership
    d. talking foolishly

5. The man's face showed only an animal **wariness**:
    a. disregard for what is right
    b. calmness of mind
    c. guarding against danger\ deception
    d. disregard for one's own safety

6. Daniel **scowled** up against the noonday sun:
    a. uttered a prayer of blessing
    b. ignored
    c. gazed contentedly
    d. made a frowning expression of displeasure

7. The large man's black skin was **mottled** with purplish bruises and patches of mud:
    a. a total lack of light
    b. marked with spots of different color
    c. partial shadow surrounding a dark center
    d. cut off at the mid-point

8. Rosh asked the man if he didn't know when he was in luck, but the man just stared down at him, **uncomprehending**:
    a. having a calmness of mind
    b. disregarding what is right
    c. not understanding
    d. having a disregard for one's own safety

9. As Daniel worked on the manacles, after an **interminable** time a narrow channel sank almost through the first band:
    a. tiresomely long; seemingly without end
    b. overwrought with pain
    c. filled with anxiety
    d. having deep remorse

10. Joel said that he meant to get the other arm of the man Daniel had, but the man's "**plagued** mule" got in the way:
    a. weak and ineffective
    b. cunning and deceitful
    c. bold and adventurous
    d. causing annoyance; a nuisance

III. Matching: Place the letter of the correct answer in the blank:

1.____bar   A. to be covered or thick with or as if with bristles

2.____unreconciled   B. a unit of the Roman army comprising 3000-6000 soldiers

3.____ruddy   C. a sharp pointed knife for stabbing

4.____flax   D. not settled or resolved

5.____tetrarch   E. knotty or misshapen

6.____legionaries   F. an accomplice or lackey who aids in the commission of disreputable acts

7.____contempt   G. of a healthy reddish complexion

8.____lurching   H. shackles for the hand or wrist

9.____dagger   I. son of

10.___livid   J. one of four joint rulers

11.___jackals   K. open disrespect for a person or thing

12.___bristling   L. fiber that is made into thread & woven into linen

13.___manacles   M. discolored by bruising

14.___gnarled   N. walking unsteadily

ANSWERS VOCABULARY TEST CHAPTERS 1-2
THE BRONZE BOW

I.   **Fill in the Blank:**

1. cranny
2. lured
3. diverted
4. vouch
5. treacherous
6. indifferent
7. draught
8. ferocity
9. stupor
10. trifle

II.   **Multiple Choice:**

1. c
2. b
3. d
4. b
5. c
6. d
7. b
8. c
9. a
10. d

III.   **Matching:**

1. I
2. D
3. G
4. L
5. J
6. B
7. K
8. N
9. C
10. M
11. F
12. A
13. H
14. E

VOCABULARY TEST CHAPTERS 3-6
THE BRONZE BOW

I. **Matching: Place the letter of the correct answer in the blank:**

1.____baffled   A. feeling or caused to feel uneasy or self-conscious

2.____jibes   B. contemptuous boldness or disregard for others

3.____impassive   C. conspicuously or grossly unconventional or unusual

4.____pilfered   D. one of the 10 divisions of a Roman legion = 300-600 men

5.____affably   E. taunting, heckling, or jeering remarks

6.____chagrined   F. prayer shawl worn by Jews at morning prayer

7.____Torah   G. showing no signs of feeling, emotion or interest

8.____tallith   H. perplexed by many conflicting situations or statements

9.____outlandish   I. courteous and agreeable in conversation

10._____phylacteries   J. arousing desire for something unattainable or out of reach

11._____tantalizing   K. to steal in small quantities

12._____cohort   L. the whole body of Jewish sacred writings & traditions

13._____impudent   M. small square leather boxes with scripture worn on the
left arm and forehead by Jewish men

ANSWERS VOCABULARY TEST CHAPTERS 3-6
THE BRONZE BOW

I.   Matching:

1. H
2. E
3. G
4. K
5. I
6. A
7. L
8. F
9. C
10. M
11. J
12. D
13. B

VOCABULARY TEST CHAPTERS 7-11
THE BRONZE BOW

I.   Multiple Choice: Circle the letter of the correct answer:

1. Rosh had a special dagger he had carried for years as a **talisman**:
    a. unwanted burden
    b. night guard
    c. sturdy walking stick
    d. an object thought to act as a charm

2. Daniel tried to crowd back the fear that rose up inside him at the sight of Leah's **disheveled** appearance:
    a. startled
    b. well-groomed
    c. extremely disorderly
    d. dull

3. Word of Daniel's **exploit** in Capernaum had reached the cave days before:
    a. strong rebuke
    b. defeat
    c. discovery
    d. notable or heroic act

4. Daniel kicked open the door to the house and let fresh air into the damp, **fetid** room:
    a. broken-down
    b. stinking
    c. ancient
    d. festive

5. Daniel **inveigled** Leah into taking one look through the door at the litter that had been prepared for her:
    a. forced
    b. tricked
    c. enticed
    d. instructed

6. The most **trivial** sound could reduce Leah to helplessness:
    a. of little importance
    b. unexpected
    c. sudden
    d. bombastic

7. Daniel did not eat as well as he had on the mountain, where meat from the farmers' flocks was free for the **plundering**:
    a. sharing
    b. recovering what is lost
    c. development
    d. taking goods by force or wrongfully

8. An accident had sent Rosh's dagger hurtling into a **chasm**:
    a. mountain lake
    b. thorny bush
    c. deep opening in the earth's surface
    d. slab of rock

9. When Jesus moved through the crowd, there was a **frenzy** of wailing, shouting, pleading voices:
    a. feeling of complete indifference
    b. violent mental agitation or wild excitement
    c. bitter hostility
    d. foolish talk

10. As Daniel and Joel talked about Rosh, they trembled at the **immensity** of the secret they shared:
    a. very great in size or degree
    b. incapable of being divided
    c. immeasurably small
    d. imperceptibly increasing

II.   Matching: Place the letter of the correct answer in the blank:

1.____quarries   A. a state of uncertainty; doubt

2.____avenge   B. an expression of disapproval

3.____toiling   C. rolling

4.____disputed   D. weaving instrument – passes horizontal threads through vertical

5.____reproach   E. afflict punishment or penalty in return for a wrong; revenge

6.____clamor   F. control or the exercise of control

7.____sullenly   G. surface excavation for the extracting of stone or slate

8.____despair   H. to rescue from destruction

9.____dominion   I. a loud continuous noise

10.___trundling   J. provoked; aroused

11.___shackles   K. proceeding with great effort

12.___salvage   L. utter loss of hope

13.___piqued   M. to deny the truth or rightness of

14.___suspicion   N. restraints that confine or restrict freedom

15.___shuttle   O. gloomily silent

ANSWERS VOCABULARY TEST CHAPTERS 7-11
THE BRONZE BOW

I. **Multiple Choice:**

   1. d
   2. c
   3. d
   4. b
   5. c
   6. a
   7. d
   8. c
   9. b
   10. a

II. **Matching:**

   1. G
   2. E
   3. K
   4. M
   5. B
   6. I
   7. O
   8. L
   9. F
   10. C
   11. N
   12. H
   13. J
   14. A
   15. D

VOCABULARY TEST CHAPTERS 12-14
THE BRONZE BOW

I.   Matching: Place the letter of the correct answer in the blank:

1.____scythe

2.____waning

3.____surly

4.____savoring

5.____disdain

6.____whetting

7.____warily

8.____recompense

9.____enchanted

10.___intricacy

11.___scandalous

12.___disconcerted

13.___flout

A. lack of respect with feeling of intense dislike

B. thrown into confusion

C. influenced as by charms or incantations

D. growing gradually smaller or less

E. careful in guarding against danger or deception

F. treat with contemptuous disregard

G. taste appreciatively

H. shocking

I. mowing implement with curved single-edged blade & long handle

J. make keen or more acute

K. payment or reward (as for services rendered)

L. a rude unfriendly disposition

M. having elaborately complex detail

ANSWER VOCABULARY TEST CHAPTERS 12-14
THE BRONZE BOW

I.   Matching:

1. I
2. D
3. L
4. G
5. A
6. J
7. E
8. K
9. C
10. M
11. H
12. B
13. F

VOCABULARY TEST CHAPTERS 15-16
THE BRONZE BOW

I.   **Fill in the Blank: Fill in the blank with the correct vocabulary word from the word bank at the end of this section:**

1. It puzzled Daniel that this timid creature who had never dared to _____ beyond their garden patch should be curious about city life.

2. Joel told Daniel that Herod Antipas was entertaining a special _____ from Rome.

3. As they made their plans, Joel's eyes sparkled at the thought of _____.

4. Daniel was not sure their plan was safe, but as he listened to the enthusiasm of Joel and Thacia, his _____ melted.

5. Joel had arranged for a _____ of fish to sell to the slaves of the centurion.

6. As they reached the milestone, the Roman soldiers could have asked them to carry their burdens another mile, but Thacia's pace had become _____.

7. As they were walking home, Thacia pointed out to Daniel hundreds of cranes passing in a great _____.

Word Bank:
scruples	legation	consignment
venture	intrigue	phalanx irksome

II. Matching: Place the letter of the correct word in the blank:

1.____glimpsed   A. stingy in giving or spending

2.____eluded   B. unduly lavish; wasteful

3.____earnestness   C. looked briefly

4.____toady   D. gleaming with or as if with brilliant light; radiant

5.____lustrous   E. a careful looking over

6.____relishing   F. try to gain favor by cringing or flattering

7.____niggardly   G. escaped, either physically or mentally

8.____reasserted   H. take pleasure in; enjoy

9.____extravagant   I. seriously intent and sober

10.___scrutiny   J. strengthen or make more firm

ANSWERS VOCABULARY TEST CHAPTERS 15-16
THE BRONZE BOW

I.   Fill in the blank:

1. venture
2. legation
3. intrigue
4. scruples
5. consignment
6. irksome
7. phalanx

II.   Matching:

1. C
2. G
3. I
4. F
5. D
6. H
7. A
8. J
9. B
10. E

VOCABULARY TEST CHAPTERS 17-24
THE BRONZE BOW

I. Multiple Choice: Circle the letter of the correct answer:

1. A bridal party on its way to Sepphoris found themselves **bereft** of their cloaks, their gifts and almost their senses:
    a. full
    b. left money under a will
    c. deprived
    d. careless

2. Daniel and his friends felt that those who **patronized** a Roman theater were fair prey:
    a. refused to do business with
    b. stayed away from
    c. owned jointly
    d. supported or sponsored

3. Daniel found a spot where a **fissure** extended down the face of the rock:
    a. hole
    b. narrow opening or crack
    c. curved knife
    d. parade of soldiers

4. Simon told Daniel the priests were trying to trap Jesus into saying something they can prove is **blasphemy**:
    a. showing irreverence for God
    b. showing irreverence for one's country
    c. showing reverence for one's country
    d. showing reverence for God

5. Daniel looked at the circle of intense **swarthy** faces:
    a. cold
    b. dark in color or complexion
    c. hearty
    d. vigorously expressive

6. Daniel told Marcus that even if he could save Leah's life, he would not allow the Roman to **profane** their house:
    a. uphold the sacredness of
    b. set apart for religious purposes
    c. violate the sacredness of
    d. cease to use for religious purposes

7. While everyone was celebrating the Day of Atonement, Daniel worked **dourly** through the morning:
    a. silently ill-humored; gloomy
    b. deliberately provocative
    c. pleasingly appropriate
    d. happily

8. Daniel told Leah, "Stop **groveling** and listen to me:"
    a. being overbearingly loud
    b. behaving in a servile or demeaning manner
    c. arousing laughter
    d. behaving graciously self-assured

9. With a wail, Leah went down on her knees, **scrabbling** on the floor for an orange:
    a. leaping gracefully
    b. rolling noisily
    c. scraping or groping frantically with hands
    d. making a careful record

10. When Daniel found Jesus, the crowd was making such a roar that he thought no one could make himself heard over such a **tumult**:
    a. state of commotion, noise & confusion
    b. spiritual rebirth
    c. secret alliance
    d. rhythmic beat

II.   Matching: Place the letter of the correct answer in the blank:

1.____defrauded   A. defeated decisively

2.____indignant   B. a feeling of evil to come

3.____garnered   C. devoutly religious

4.____routed   D. having a slanting or sloping direction, course or position

5.____flaunted   E. deprived of by deceit

6.____reprisal   F. scholars of Jewish law in New Testament times

7.____oblique   G. angered at something unjust or wrong

8.____foreboding   H. an act in retaliation for something done for another

9.____scribes   I. to assemble or get together

10.___pious   J. to show off

III.   Matching: Place the letter of the correct answer in the blank:

1.____frivolous   A. something created by mixing a variety of components

2.____amends   B. coming and going at intervals

3.____preoccupation   C. lacking in seriousness

4.____cowered   D. a European strong-scented herb with bitter tasting leaves

5.____averted   E. unnaturally pale, as from physical or emotional distress

6.____loathing   F. to shrink or crouch down as from fear or cold

7.____intermittent   G. extremely dry, especially by exposure to heat

8.____wan   H. compensation for injury or loss

9.____remorse   I. hate coupled with disgust

10.___parched   J. complete absorption of the mind or interests

11.___concoction   K. turned aside or away

12.___rue   L. gnawing distress arising from a sense of guilt for past wrongs

ANSWERS VOCABULARY TEST CHAPTERS 17-24
THE BRONZE BOW

I.   **Multiple Choice:**

1. c
2. d
3. b
4. a
5. b
6. c
7. a
8. b
9. c
10. a

II.   **Matching:**

1. E
2. G
3. I
4. A
5. J
6. H
7. D
8. B
9. F
10. C

III.   **Matching:**

1. C
2. H
3. J
4. F
5. K
6. I
7. B
8. E
9. L
10. G
11. A
12. D

TEST QUESTIONS
THE BRONZE BOW

I. **Multiple Choice: Circle the letter of the correct answer:**

1. The setting of this story is:
   a. Galilee in the time of Daniel the Prophet
   b. Galilee in the time of Jesus
   c. Galilee in the time of Moses
   d. Galilee in the time of Nero

2. Daniel Bar Jamin had been apprenticed to work as a:
   a. weaver
   b. shoemaker
   c. blacksmith
   d. soldier

3. When Joel and Thacia came to the mountain, Daniel shows them the plain where:
   a. Abraham won a great victory
   b. David won a great victory
   c. Moses won a great victory
   d. Joshua won a great victory

4. One of the reasons Joel had wanted to come to the mountain was:
   a. he was an avid rock climber
   b. he wanted to be closer to God
   c. hehoped to be able to meet Rosh
   d. he knew Daniel was there

5. When Joel tells Rosh of his desire, Rosh tells him to:
   a. go to Capernaum with his family
   b. give up all for the cause
   c. come and join them
   d. hand over all his money

6. Daniel wins the trust and gratitude of "Samson," the large slave they steal from the caravan, by:
   a. coaxing him with a large meal
   b. talking to him as he takes his shackles off
   c. freeing him from Rosh
   d. telling him what a great friend he is

7. Daniel receives a visit from:
   a. his grandmother
   b. Joel's father
   c. his uncle
   d. Simon the Zealot

8. One of the things that has happened to Daniel while he has been living on the mountain with Rosh is:
   a. he has not been faithful to God's laws
   b. he has received daily news from Ketzah
   c. he is closer to God than before
   d. he forgotwhat he knew of his trade

9. When Daniel first sees Jesus in the synagogue and hears Him speak:
   a. he becomes bored and falls asleep
   b. he runs out screaming
   c. his spirit is stirred; he feels excited
   d. he hides from him

10. On his way home from the synagogue, Daniel almost causes trouble for the whole village by:
   a. starting a riot
   b. taunting a young boy
   c. picking someone's pocket
   d. throwing a rock at a soldier

11. When Daniel asks Rosh about going to Capernaum to find Joel, Rosh tell him:
   a. Joel probably has forgotten him
   b. he has been wanting him to find Joel
   c. Joel may be too rich to join them
   d. too much work on the mountain

12. Daniel's relationship with Joel and Thacia is radically changed when he:
    a. becomes wounded
    b. finds out he is a relative
    c. is captured by the Romans
    d. moves closer to their home

13. Joel spends time reading to Daniel and Thacia from:
    a. the newspaper
    b. letters from his grandmother
    c. Moby Dick
    d. Scripture

14. After Daniel relates how his parents died, Joel and Thacia:
    a. ask their father if he will adopt Daniel
    b. help him find a counseling group
    c. take an oath for God's Victory vs Rome
    d. send Daniel away

15. As Daniel breaks the Law by traveling on the Sabbath, he rationalizes this by telling himself:
    a. the Law is only for the rich
    b. there is no law against traveling
    c. he won't be going too far
    d. he's pretty good for the most part, anyway

16. After Daniel's first "solo" assignment for Rosh, Rosh tells Daniel he has:
    a. a mean streak
    b. a greedy streak
    c. a soft streak
    d. a funny streak

17. When Daniel receives a message that his grandmother is dying and goes into the village, he finds the neighbors outside the locked door because:
    a. they are afraid of getting sick
    b. they think his sister is demon-possessed
    c. his sister is under house arrest
    d. no one has a key

18. As Daniel ministers to his grandmother, he:
    a. tells her of his work on the mountain
    b. sings songs
    c. sits with her without talking
    d. talks about verses she taught them

19. In order to provide for Leah and himself, Simon tells Daniel:
    a. he can come and work as his assistant
    b. he will help him find a job
    c. he can take over his shop and house
    d. he will have to beg in the streets

20. When Daniel meets Nathan:
    a. he has been beaten up by several boys
    b. he is chained by the Romanas
    c. Nathan has beaten up several boys
    d. he is working for Rosh

21. After Daniel meets Nathan:
    a. Nathan is his only friend
    b. Joel comes bringing Kemuel
    c. Joktan comes and joins him
    d. Daniel introduces Nathan to Leah

22. After Thacia visits Leah the first time, Daniel realizes:
    a. he has neglected feeding Leah properly
    b. he needs to give Leah more work to do
    c. he has neglected Leah's clothing
    d. Leah and Thacia are alike

23. When Daniel returns to the mountain for a night, one indication he is changing is:
    a. he has forgotten the password
    b. Rosh doesn't know him
    c. the jokes are not so funny
    d. he feels guilty about taking farmer's sheep

24. The summer month of Ab is happiest for Daniel because:
    a. he goes on vacation
    b. the Romans leave
    c. he sees Jesus, Joel and Thacia every day
    d. he sees Rosh everyday

25. The parable that Daniel has the hardest time understanding is that of:
    a. The Good Samaritan
    b. The Mustard Seed
    c. The Wheat and the Tares
    d. The Sower and the Seed

26. As Daniel sees Leah changing and becoming stronger, he believes this is the result of:
    a. his influence in Leah's life
    b. Thacia's influence
    c. Joel's influence
    d. the influence of the Roman soldier

27. Daniel gives Thacia:
    a. a wedding ring
    b. a new dress
    c. a garland of flowers for her hair
    d. a bronze brooch like a bow & arrow

28. After Joel obtains information for Rosh, Rosh uses the information:
    a. to defeat the Romans
    b. to spy on Herod
    c. to steal from other Jews
    d. build a case against Jesus

29. When Daniel goes to Rosh for help after Joel is arrested by the Romans, Daniel discovers:
    a. Rosh will do anything to help his men
    b. Rosh will not help to rescue Joel
    c. Rosh has influence with the jailor
    d. Rosh gives instructions to follow

30. Joel asks Daniel to get a message to Jesus that:
    a. Herod and his men were trying to kill Him
    b. the Romans want to kill Him
    c. synagogue elders want to kill Him
    d. Pontius Pilate wants to kill Him

31. When he returns from the celebration for the Day of Atonement, Daniel finds out that Leah's improvement has been aided by:
    a. her friendship with Thacia
    b. her friendship with Joktan
    c. her friendship with Joel
    d. her friendship the Roman soldier

32. Daniel's reaction to Leah's revelation causes her to:
    a. return to her former state
    b. run away from home
    c. become more bold
    d. decide to become a Roman

33. When Leah becomes ill and is fighting for her life, the person who is most grieved by her illness and stands watch constantly to find out how she is doing is:
    a. Daniel
    b. Marcus
    c. Thacia
    d. Joel

34. When Leah awakens, she tells Daniel she knows she must feel the same as:
    a. the Emperor's daughter
    b. Herod's daughter
    c. Jairus' daughter
    d. Moses' daughter

35. Daniel understands the courage it takes to follow Jesus when he is able to win the battle:
    a. against Marcus by beating him
    b. against hatred by being kind to Marcus
    c. against all the Romans
    d. against Herod

II.   Matching: Place the letter of the correct answer in the blank:

1.____Daniel bar Jamin   A. gave his life for Daniel because of his gratitude

2.____Leah   B. rich girl who could make herself fit in to any situation

3.____Joel bar Hezron   C. the first recruit in the village for Daniel's "army"

4.____Malthace   D. living far away from home & thankful for kindness from Leah

5.____Rosh   E. blacksmith who became a disciple of Jesus

6.____Marcus   F. isolation allowed this person to have no prejudices

7.____Samson   G. criminal who tried to look like a savior

8.____Joktan   H. young man whose anger at injustice caused him to be prejudiced

9.____Nathan   I. former member of robber band who becomes blacksmith apprentice

10.___Simon the Zealot   J. scholar studying to be a rabbi; has love of country & adventure

III. Matching: Place the letter of the correct answer in the blank:

1.____bronze bow   A. Thacia compares Leah to this

2.____manacles   B. Daniel got into trouble with a Roman soldier for misusing this

3.____catapult   C. Daniel described one in detail for Leah

4.____fish   D. symbolic of slavery or imprisonment

5.____bowl of water   E. the last living thing Leah has to love

6.____Day of Atonement   F. taken from 2 Sam 22:35

7.____goat   G. used by Joel to gain access to the centurion's kitchen

8.____love   H. holiday observed by the Jews – Daniel watches Thacia dance

9.____flower   I. Daniel & his band take one apart & hide it

10.___wedding   J. what Jesus demands of those who follow Him

III. Short Answer:

1. Choose two characters from the book, and compare (tell how they are alike) and contrast (tell how they are different) them.

2. In the story, Daniel is angry because of the Roman occupation of his land. Think of a modern issue that might make people angry (abortion, racial prejudice, religious persecution, gender prejudice, etc.). Explain how this issue can be handled in a way that is consistent with what Jesus teaches about dealing with people. What can you, as a young person, do about this issue right now?

3. In literature, characters who change in the course of a story are dynamic, while those who do not are static. Of the main characters in this book, which do you think are the most dynamic? Why? Which are the most static? Why?

4. Jesus said, "He who lives by the sword dies by the sword." How is this somewhat ironic in Daniel's life?

ANSWERS TEST QUESTIONS
THE BRONZE BOW

I.   Multiple Choice:

1. b
2. c
3. d
4. c
5. a
6. b
7. d
8. a
9. c
10. d
11. c
12. a
13. d
14. c
15. a
16. c
17. b
18. d
19. c
20. a
21. b
22. c
23. d
24. c
25. a
26. b
27. d
28. c
29. b
30. c
31. d
32. a
33. b
34. c
35. b

II.   Matching:

1. H
2. F
3. J
4. B
5. G
6. D
7. A
8. I

9. C

10. E

III. Matching:

1. F
2. D
3. I
4. G
5. B
6. H
7. E
8. J
9. A
10. C

IV. Short Answer:

1. Answers will vary

2. Answers will vary

3. Dynamic Characters: Daniel and Leah are the most dynamic in the story. Daniel changes from the angry young man living with criminals to a responsible tradesman who changes even more radically after his encounter with Jesus. Leah changes from a cringing, trembling girl who can barely speak to a young lady who is able to befriend a lonely Roman soldier and make him feel that not everyone in this country is antagonistic to him.
Static Characters: Although Joel and Thacia undergo some changes, for the most part they are static characters who are there for the sake of contrast to Daniel and Leah. There is little difference in their character at the end of the story from the beginning. Rosh is also a static character, never changing throughout the story at all.

4. Although Daniel thought it would be glorious to die on the battlefield fighting for his country, he finds instead that the sword pierces his heart with guilt when he feels responsible for the deaths of Nathan and Samson, rather than seeing himself die in the fighting.

Bronze Bow Vocab Chapt 1-2 A

Across

5. sharp pointed knife for stabbing
10. son of
11. a small opening, as in a wall or rock face; a crevice
13. not settled or resolved
15. draw on with a promise of pleasure or gain
16. turned from a course or purpose
18. extremely nervous; tense
19. cause of annoyance; a nuisance
20. give a guarantee

Down

1. a unit of the Roman army comprising 3000 to 6000 soldiers
2. dangerously unstable and unpredictable
3. love of country and willingness to sacrifice for it
4. a noisy, disorderly fight or quarrel; a brawl
6. growing and flourishing
7. open disrespect for a person or thing
8. fiber of the flax plant that is made into thread and woven into linen fabric
9. made a frowning expression of displeasure
12. walking unsteadily
14. one of four joint rulers
17. of a healthy reddish complexion

Bronze Bow Vocab Chapt 1-2 A

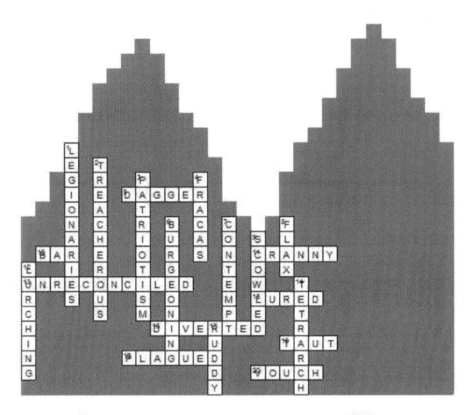

Across

5. sharp pointed knife for stabbing
10. son of
11. a small opening, as in a wall or rock face; a crevice
13. not settled or resolved
15. draw on with a promise of pleasure or gain
16. turned from a course or purpose
18. extremely nervous; tense
19. cause of annoyance; a nuisance
20. give a guarantee

Down

1. a unit of the Roman army comprising 3000 to 6000 soldiers
2. dangerously unstable and unpredictable
3. love of country and willingness to sacrifice for it
4. a noisy, disorderly fight or quarrel; a brawl
6. growing and flourishing
7. open disrespect for a person or thing
8. fiber of the flax plant that is made into thread and woven into linen fabric
9. made a frowning expression of displeasure
12. walking unsteadily
14. one of four joint rulers
17. of a healthy reddish complexion

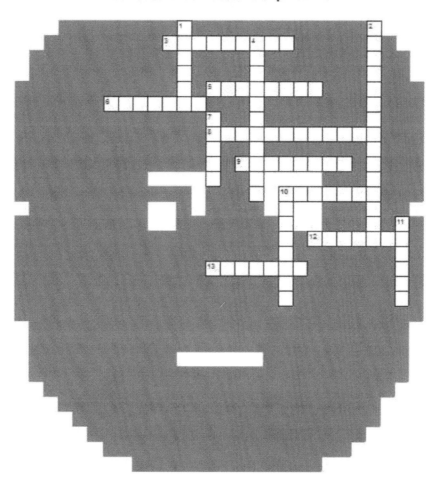

Bronze Bow Vocab Chapt 1-2 B

Across

3. covered or thick with or as if with bristles
5. careful in guarding against danger or deception
6. knotty or misshapen
8. tiresomely long; seemingly without end
9. wild and turbulent
10. marked with spots of different color
12. a serving of drink drawn from a keg
13. accomplices or lackeys who aid in the commission of base or disreputable acts

Down

1. something of little value or importance
2. not understanding
4. of no importance one way or another
7. discolored by bruising
10. shackles for the hand or wrist
11. a state of extreme apathy or torpor often following stress or shock

Bronze Bow Vocab Chapt 1-2 B

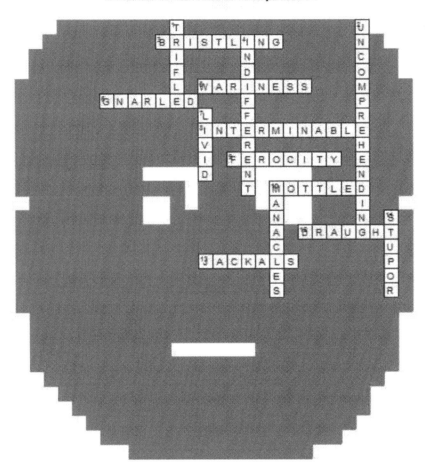

Across

3. covered or thick with or as if with bristles
5. careful in guarding against danger or deception
6. knotty or misshapen
8. tiresomely long; seemingly without end
9. wild and turbulent
10. marked with spots of different color
12. a serving of drink drawn from a keg
13. accomplices or lackeys who aid in the commission of base or disreputable acts

Down

1. something of little value or importance
2. not understanding
4. of no importance one way or another
7. discolored by bruising
10. shackles for the hand or wrist
11. a state of extreme apathy or torpor often following stress or shock

Bronze Bow Vocab Chapt 3-6

Across

5. conspicuously or grossly unconventional or unusual
7. a shawl with ritually knotted fringe at each corner, worn by Jews at morning prayer
9. arousing desire or expectation of something unattainable or mockingly out of reach
12. taunting, heckling, or jeering remarks
13. perplexed by many conflicting situations or statements

Down

1. contemptuous boldness or disregard of others
2. showing no signs of feeling, emotion, or interest
3. one of the 10 divisions of a Roman legion , consisting of 300 to 600 men
4. small square leather boxes containing slips inscribed with Scripture passages and traditionally worn on the left arm and forehead by Jewish men
6. feeling or causing to feel uneasy and self-conscious
8. to steal in small quantities
10. courteous and agreeable in conversation
11. the whole body of the Jewish sacred writings and tradition including the oral tradition

Bronze Bow Vocab Chapt 3-6

Across

5. conspicuously or grossly unconventional or unusual
7. a shawl with ritually knotted fringe at each corner; worn by Jews at morning prayer
9. arousing desire or expectation of something unattainable or mockingly out of reach
12. taunting, heckling, or jeering remarks
13. perplexed by many conflicting situations or statements

Down

1. contemptuous boldness or disregard of others
2. showing no signs of feeling, emotion, or interest
3. one of the 10 divisions of a Roman legion , consisting of 300 to 600 men
4. small square leather boxes containing slips inscribed with Scripture passages and traditionally worn on the left arm and forehead by Jewish men
6. feeling or causing to feel uneasy and self-conscious
8. to steal in small quantities
10. courteous and agreeable in conversation
11. the whole body of the Jewish sacred writings and tradition including the oral tradition

Bronze Bow Vocab Chapt 7-11

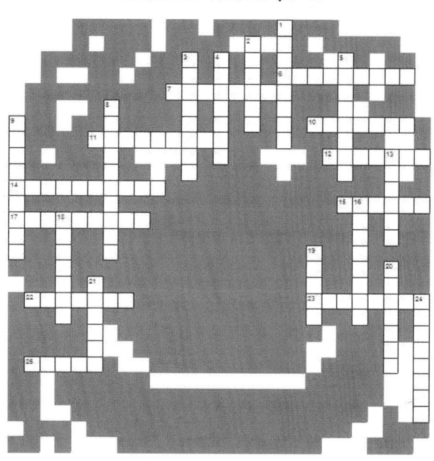

Across

6. win over by flattery; entice
7. an object thought to act as a charm
10. an instrument used in weaving for passing the horizontal threads between the vertical threads
11. a state of uncertainty; doubt
12. utter loss of hope
14. in disarray; extremely disorderly
15. a state of violent mental agitation or wild excitement
17. very great in size or degree
22. of little importance
23. restraints that confine or restrict freedom
25. having an offensive smell; stinking

Down

1. control of the exercise of control
2. a loud continuous noise
3. a surface excavation for extracting stone or slate
4. proceed with great effort
5. denied the truth or rightness of
8. take the goods of by force or wrongfully
9. rolling
13. inflict a punishment or penalty in return for a wrong
16. an expression of disapproval
18. a notable or heroic act
19. a deep opening in the earth's surface
20. rescue from destruction
21. provoked; aroused
24. gloomily silent

Bronze Bow Vocab Chapt 7-11

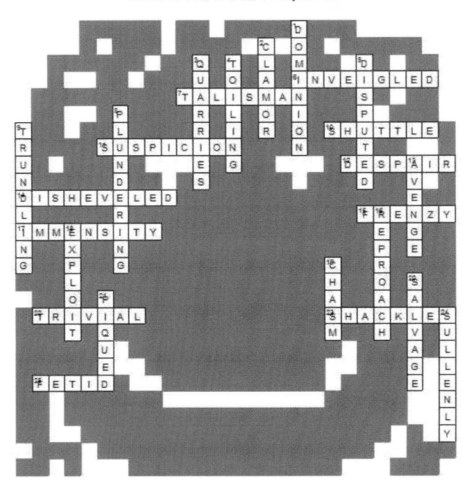

Across

6. win over by flattery; entice
7. an object thought to act as a charm
10. an instrument used in weaving for passing the horizontal threads between the vertical threads
11. a state of uncertainty; doubt
12. utter loss of hope
14. in disarray; extremely disorderly
15. a state of violent mental agitation or wild excitement
17. very great in size or degree
22. of little importance
23. restraints that confine or restrict freedom
25. having an offensive smell; stinking

Down

1. control of the exercise of control
2. a loud continuous noise
3. a surface excavation for extracting stone or slate
4. proceed with great effort
5. denied the truth or rightness of
8. take the goods of by force or wrongfully
9. rolling
13. inflict a punishment or penalty in return for a wrong
16. an expression of disapproval
18. a notable or heroic act
19. a deep opening in the earth's surface
20. rescue from destruction
21. provoked; aroused
24. gloomily silent

Bronze Bow Vocab Chapt 12-14

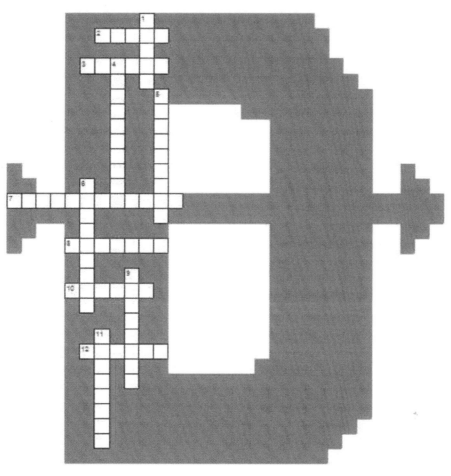

Across

2. treat with contemptuous disregard
3. careful in guarding against danger or deception
7. thrown into confusion
8. lack of respect accompanied by a feeling of intense dislike
10. an implement consisting of a long,curved, single-edged blade with a long bent handle reaping
12. growing gradually smaller or less

Down

1. rude unfriendly disposition
4. payment or reward (as for service)
5. influenced by charms or incantations
6. having elaborately complex detail
9. making keen or more acute
11. tasting appreciatively

Bronze Bow Vocab Chapt 12-14

```
                    S
           F L O U T
                    R
         W A R I L Y
             E      Y
             C        E
             O        N
             M        C
             P        H
             E        A
             N        N
         I   S        T
   D I S C O N C E R T E D
         T            D
         R
       D I S D A I N
         C      W
       S C Y T H E
         Y      E
                T
         S      T
       W A N I N G
         V      N
         O      G
         R
         I
         N
         G
```

Across

2. treat with contemptuous disregard
3. careful in guarding against danger or deception
7. thrown into confusion
8. lack of respect accompanied by a feeling of intense dislike
10. an implement consisting of a long, curved, single-edged blade with a long bent handle reaping
12. growing gradually smaller or less

Down

1. rude unfriendly disposition
4. payment or reward (as for service)
5. influenced by charms or incantations
6. having elaborately complex detail
9. making keen or more acute
11. tasting appreciatively

Bronze Bow Vocab Chapt 15-16

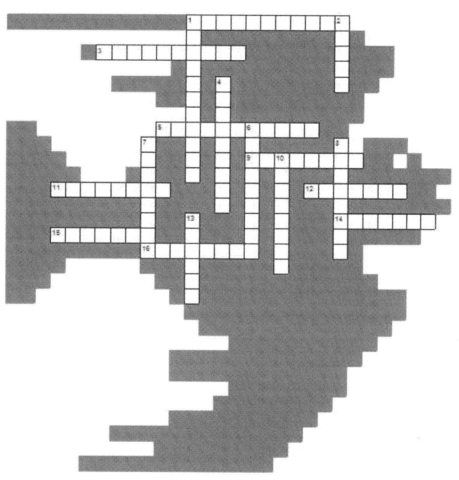

Across

1. unduly lavish; wasteful
3. strengthen or make more firm
5. the delivery of goods for sale or disposal
9. looked briefly; glanced
11. gleaming with or as if with brilliant light; radiant
12. a group or body in compact formation
14. causing annoyance, weariness, or vexation; tedious
15. proceed somewhere despite the risk of possible dangers
16. a careful looking over

Down

1. seriously intent and sober
2. try to gain favor by cringing or flattering
4. take pleasure in; enjoy
6. stingy in giving or spending
7. an uneasy feeling arising from conscience or principle that tends to hinder action
8. a diplomatic mission headed by a minister
10. a secret scheme
13. escaped, either physically or mentally

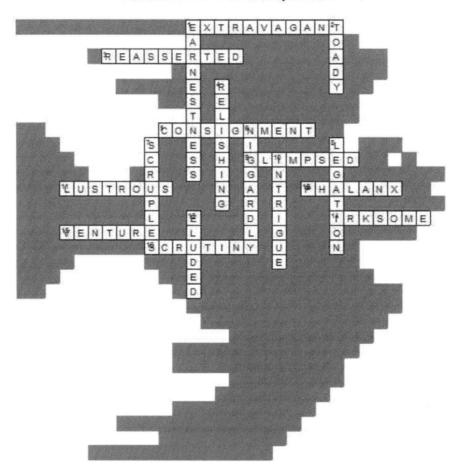

Bronze Bow Vocab Chapt 15-16

Across

1. unduly lavish; wasteful
3. strengthen or make more firm
5. the delivery of goods for sale or disposal
9. looked briefly; glanced
11. gleaming with or as if with brilliant light; radiant
12. a group or body in compact formation
14. causing annoyance, weariness, or vexation; tedious
15. proceed somewhere despite the risk of possible dangers
16. a careful looking over

Down

1. seriously intent and sober
2. try to gain favor by cringing or flattering
4. take pleasure in; enjoy
6. stingy in giving or spending
7. an uneasy feeling arising from conscience or principle that tends to hinder action
8. a diplomatic mission headed by a minister
10. a secret scheme
13. escaped, either physically or mentally

The Bronze Bow Vocab Chapt 17-24 A

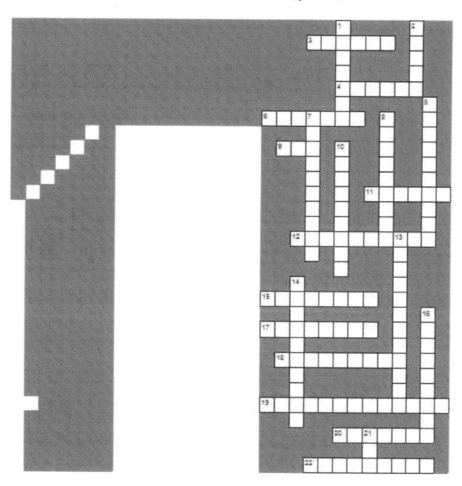

Across

3. deprived of or lacking something
4. compensation for injury or loss
6. extremely dry, especially by exposure to heat
9. unnaturally pale, as from physical or emotional distress
11. a state of commotion and noise and confusion
12. a feeling of evil to come
15. to show off
17. assemble or get together
18. angered at something unjust or wrong
19. complete absorption of the mind or interests
20. scholars of Jewish law in New Testament times
22. behave in a servile or demeaning manner; cringe

Down

1. treat something sacred with irreverence or contempt
2. devoutly religious
5. scraping or groping about frenetically with the hands
7. something created by compounding or mixing a variety of components
8. deprive of by deceit
10. the act of expressing lack or reverence for God
13. coming and going at intervals
14. to act as a patron to; support or sponsor
16. lacking in seriousness
21. a European strong-scented woody herb with bitter-tasting leaves

The Bronze Bow Vocab Chapt 17-24 A

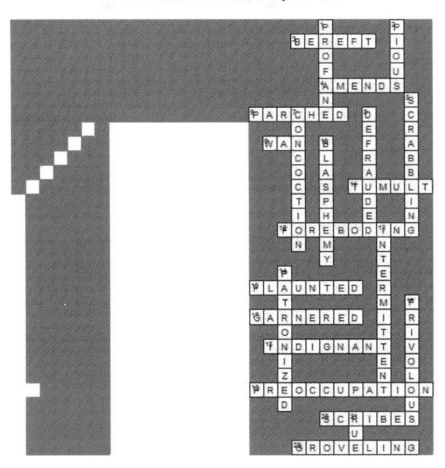

Across

3. deprived of or lacking something
4. compensation for injury or loss
6. extremely dry, especially by exposure to heat
9. unnaturally pale, as from physical or emotional distress
11. a state of commotion and noise and confusion
12. a feeling of evil to come
15. to show off
17. assemble or get together
18. angered at something unjust or wrong
19. complete absorption of the mind or interests
20. scholars of Jewish law in New Testament times
22. behave in a servile or demeaning manner; cringe

Down

1. treat something sacred with irreverence or contempt
2. devoutly religious
5. scraping or groping about frenetically with the hands
7. something created by compounding or mixing a variety of components
8. deprive of by deceit
10. the act of expressing lack or reverence for God
13. coming and going at intervals
14. to act as a patron to; support or sponsor
16. lacking in seriousness
21. a European strong-scented woody herb with bitter-tasting leaves

The Bronze Bow Vocab Chapt 17-24 B

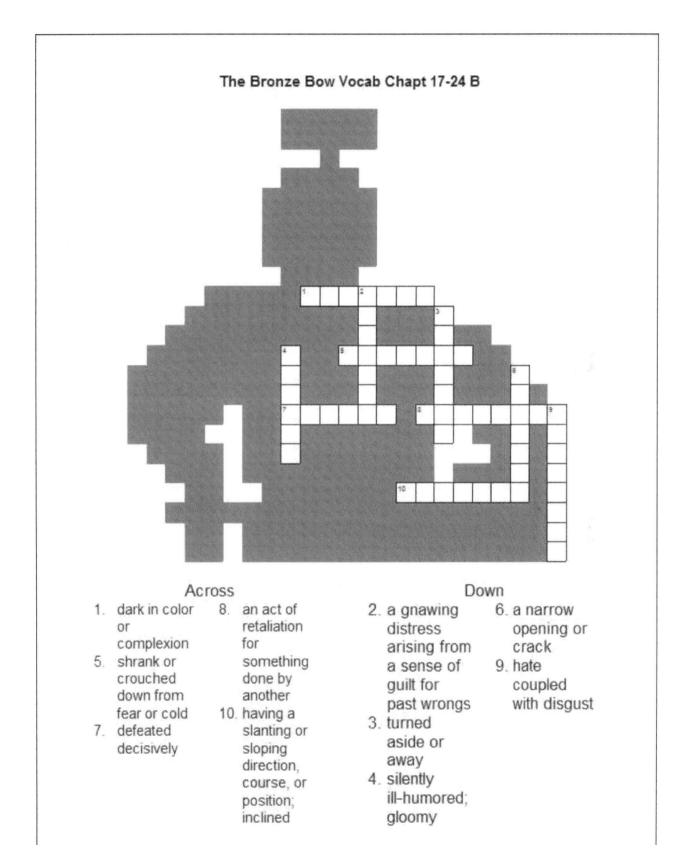

Across

1. dark in color or complexion
5. shrank or crouched down from fear or cold
7. defeated decisively
8. an act of retaliation for something done by another
10. having a slanting or sloping direction, course, or position; inclined

Down

2. a gnawing distress arising from a sense of guilt for past wrongs
3. turned aside or away
4. silently ill-humored; gloomy
6. a narrow opening or crack
9. hate coupled with disgust

The Bronze Bow Vocab Chapt 17-24 B

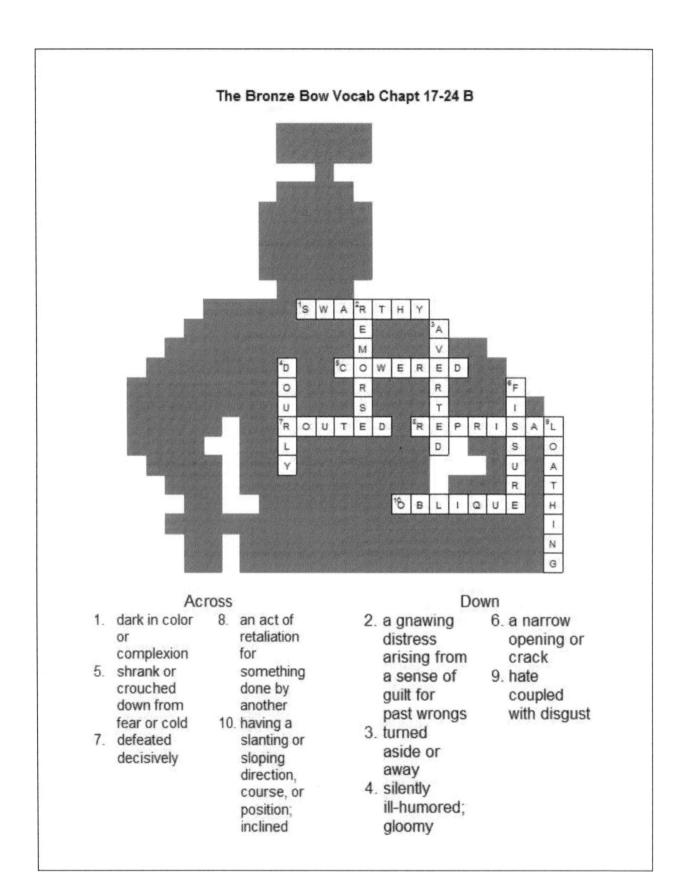

Across

1. dark in color or complexion
5. shrank or crouched down from fear or cold
7. defeated decisively
8. an act of retaliation for something done by another
10. having a slanting or sloping direction, course, or position; inclined

Down

2. a gnawing distress arising from a sense of guilt for past wrongs
3. turned aside or away
4. silently ill-humored; gloomy
6. a narrow opening or crack
9. hate coupled with disgust

SELECTED BIBLIOGRAPHY

Biographical Material

Speare, Elizabeth George.
   <http://www.edupaperback.org/showauth.cfm?authid=85.html.> 2006.

http://www.wikipedia.org/w/index.php?title=Elizabeth_George_Speare&p.html. 2006.

Background Material:

Brisco, Thomas C. Holman Bible Atlas. Nashville: Broadman and Holman. 1998.

Maier, Paul L. Josephus The Essential Works. Grand Rapids: Kregel Publications. 1988.

Dictionaries

Webster's Third International Dictionary. Springfield, MA: G & C.
   Merriam Co., 1963.

Webster's Universal College Dictionary. New York: Gramercy Books, 1997.

http://www.thefreedictionary.com/html. 2006.

Made in United States
Orlando, FL
25 June 2023